ISRAEL

ENDPAPERS The stones of old Jerusalem – from a street in the Old City

BELOW *Yom Hashoa* (Holocaust Memorial Day), 8 a.m. A siren marks a two-minute silence

OVERLEAF The Negev

ISRAEL

FREDERIC BRENNER AND A.B.YEHOSHUA

Translated from the Hebrew by Philip Simpson

COLLINS HARVILL
8 Grafton Street, London W1
1988

William Collins Sons and Co Ltd
London · Glasgow · Sydney · Auckland
Toronto · Johannesburg

British Library Cataloguing in Publication Data
Brenner, Frédéric, *1959–*
Israel.
1. Israel
I. Title II. Yehoshua, A.B. (Avraham B.)
1936–
956.94'054
ISBN 0-00-271347-0

First published by Collins Harvill 1988

Designed by Ronald Clark
Photoset in Itek Meridien by
Ace Filmsetting Ltd, Frome, Somerset
Colour and duotone origination by
Amilcare Pizzi SpA, Milan
Printed and bound in Italy by
Amilcare Pizzi SpA, Milan

CONTENTS

PHOTOGRAPHS ON FOLLOWING PAGES

Pages 10–11 Massada

Pages 12–13 Near Hebron

Pages 14–15 Mount Hermon and the Golan Heights from the Circassian village of Rihaniya, Upper Galilee

INTRODUCTION

TO BE HAPPY?

This is the question. In order that our nature may be changed as far as is possible, we need an environment of our own, and so that we may create this environment with our own hands – our nature must be utterly changed.

Y. H. BRENNER

"Do the Jews really want just to be happy?" the Jewish-German philosopher Hermann Cohen incredulously asked his friend, the great philosopher Martin Buber, in Germany in the early years of this century. Buber was trying to persuade him to join the Zionist movement. "Must we really abandon Europe, the centre of world culture, betray the great mission of the Jewish people, a mission that is moral and religious and beset by suffering, in order to establish another Albania in the Middle East?" Hermann Cohen concluded.

These were the early days of the famous Golden Age of Jewish-German symbiosis which reached its peak in the 1920s. Native-born German Jews and émigrés from Eastern Europe had begun to make a real contribution to German art and culture after the country's defeat in the First World War. They did so not only because they wished to assimilate a profound tradition but with a vision of historic cooperation and cross-fertilization between two peoples; philosophers like Cohen and Franz Rosenzweig even envisaged a distinctive Jewish-German strand in Western culture. The same period saw the collapse of Tsarist Russia and the triumph of the October Revolution, to which many Jews subscribed in the belief that equality in a classless society would greatly alleviate their suffering. The American continent was opening its doors to the first waves of immigration and millions of Jews turned from the East to a new life in the West where an individual was measured not by birthright, religion or nationality but by talent and achievement, and where a constitution guaranteed him freedom and equality before the law. In Palestine, four centuries of Turkish rule were coming to an end as the British advanced on Jerusalem. On 2 November 1917, the Balfour Declaration promised the Jews a national home in the ancient land of their fathers.

The new democracies of Western and Central Europe encouraged Jews to take an active part in political and cultural life. Jews began to feel that history might at last be working in their favour. New doors were opening; acceptance and assimilation seemed only a few years away. But it was never to be. Within fifteen years the wheel began to turn backwards with horrifying results. Doors that had beckoned so welcomingly were closed one after another; some proved to be not doors but traps, others were the gates of Hell itself. The door of emigration to America was shut tight by the Great Depression. The door of the October Revolution slammed shut, cutting off millions of Jews from family and custom elsewhere. In Palestine, Arab opposition to Zionism persuaded the British to curtail immigration. Worst of all, in the heart of Europe, Fascism and Nazism were born. Within a few years half the Jews in the world were doomed to wander the circles of Hell, drifting ever downwards, and Hermann Cohen's idealized spiritual suffering became a suffering the like of which had never been known in history. Uprooted from their homes, persecuted beyond endurance, families torn apart, interned in vile concentration camps, naked and defenceless, the Jewish people arrived at the lowest circle – destroyed by gas, like an infection, by those whom a few years before they had thought partners in a new vision.

Events happened with lightning speed, and when the last clouds of smoke lifted from Europe in 1945 world Jewry faced utter ruin. Six million had been exterminated, three million more were trapped in the Soviet Union. Traumatized by the Holocaust and now stateless, hundreds of thousands of people began searching for their "Albania" which, if it did not give them happiness, might at least provide a roof over their heads. The stunned remnants of the Jewish people turned southeast towards the only door that had not been completely closed, which their brothers who had preceded them in the 1920s had managed to keep ajar.

Sometimes the moral imperative can triumph over immediate interests. In 1947, at the height of the Cold War, the United Nations adopted a plan to partition Palestine and establish a Jewish state. Both East and West (and especially Europeans) were profoundly shocked by the pathological destruction that had been inflicted on the Jews. They joined forces to resolve the Jewish problem, to provide a place where Jews could live alone, under their own rule, and be *like all other nations*.

Revolutions are always the work of a handful of people, but never was a national revolution conducted in such isolation, so apart from those it would ultimately affect, never was a revolution conducted under such dangerous conditions. The Zionist adventure could easily have ended in disaster, aborted physically and economically by the Arabs. The thousands of Jews who arrived in Palestine in the first three decades of this century and stayed (a great many left) were a ray of hope to world Jewry after the Holocaust. The Zionists of the early twentieth century laid the foundations for what was to become the Jewish state. Without these foundations, the UN Declaration in 1947 would have remained just another meaningless scrap of paper.

Israel is forty years old, and one who witnessed its birth as a babe in arms and observed its development with trepidation now sees an adult personality – but is it a normal personality? Having clung to exile through all the long centuries of the Diaspora, the Jewish people had become afraid to be like other nations, and was unable to rescue itself from the fire. Although from any perspective the last four decades are remarkable, have the Jews really succeeded at last in becoming like other nations? Are they really content now just to be happy, and if so does this bring them sadness, or joy?

CHAPTER ONE

HISTORICAL PERSPECTIVES

And I had no time
To grow a tree
Of thoughts
At my pace, slowly
Something more understood
Less a potpourri
Of shouts
Of meals taken standing.

My life went by from newspaper to newspaper
My breath was winded
In short-distance runs
For His sake.

And I had no time
To cover myself with hyssop
Or a shirt
No time for
Birth-burial-birth
To join with memories
Or for the pages of the heavy tome
To yellow.

To be understood
Certain
Lost
Gain an inheritance
Between my father and me – the sea.

HAIM GOURI

A well-known Israeli historian once told me something which astonished me at first, but which on reflection became perfectly plausible. The Jewish people has lived for hundreds if not thousands of years without historical consciousness. A people reckoned by the world to have lived entirely on its historical consciousness has in fact created for itself a nonhistorical existence in which there has been no concern with the recording, documentation, preservation and teaching of history, and least of all with its research. Because it moved from place to place, because it effectively stopped using its own language (except in the context of religious observance) and because it was not associated with long-lasting physical monuments – such as the castles and cathedrals which have perpetuated the history of many other peoples – the Jewish people lived in a metaphysical time zone containing certain key mytho-historical points, such as the Exodus from Egypt, the revelation of the Law on Mount Sinai and the destruction of the Temple (that of the First Temple in 586 BC and of the Second Temple in AD 70 being combined in a single episode).

These points were joined in a line that itself aspired to a no less extratemporal and nonhistorical point – the coming of the Messiah, final redemption and the resurrection of the dead. Note that these links are causal-religious and not historical-sociological. Thus in Jewish consciousness the destruction of the Temple could have happened only yesterday and the Messiah could be due to arrive tomorrow, or the destruction of the Temple could have happened thousands of years ago and the Messiah could come thousands of years in the future. Jews living in a remote township in Russia had no knowledge whatsoever of the existence of Jews in Morocco or Yemen; on the contrary, in a certain sense they would not have been surprised had they been told that theirs was the only Jewish community in the world. They would have reacted with the same equanimity to news of a Jewish community at the South Pole. Events were perceived according to a pre-existing model: sin — punishment — suffering — repentance — mercy — punishment of enemies and full redemption, culminating in metaphysical return to the Land. In the rabbinical schools and seminaries where they spent so much of their time, Jews were not concerned with history but with the constant exegesis of ancient texts prescribing detailed rules for the religious conduct of everyday life, rules perceived as valid for every place and every time.

The study of history among Jews first emerged at the end of the eighteenth century. It was an initiative which sought to abandon the religious framework and to engage, to a certain extent, in a new and vigorous process of assimilation into liberated European society. Members of the "Wisdom of Israel" (as this movement was called) saw it as their task to compose the definitive version of Jewish history in order to leave behind a glorious memorial to a whole culture they believed would soon be swept away by the tide of emancipation. Later, in the nineteenth century, they were followed by nationalist and secular scholars who studied Jewish history as a living organism capable of nourishing the nationalist consciousness which was then beginning to hatch from the thick and stifling shell of religious tradition.

The greatest scholar of Jewry in the twentieth century, Professor Gershon Sholem, defined Zionism as *return to history*. The definition is certainly appropriate to the devotees of Zionism, who saw this "return" as something dramatic and intense. The Jewish people was like an ageing bachelor who at fifty marries a young woman and must quickly learn the obligations which to his friends are a natural way of life; or like an adult who has never studied in a methodical way but decides to become a student and tries to obtain his BA, MA and doctorate in just a year. What other nations had managed gradually and organically, Jews needed to achieve within a few years. What might take a century or more in any other context had to be condensed into a few decades: liberation, independence, colonial struggles and perhaps even a small-scale civil war, legislative wrangles, religious feuds, the politics of immigration. As Israelis always say when times are hard: *at least in Israel life is never boring!*

It is not enough, therefore, to examine the history of the State of Israel on the basis of issues and criteria observable in similar modern states in the free world. It is essential also to recognize that behind the headlines and the problems of a new democracy there lurk the heavy shadows of ancient struggles which other nations have long since dispensed with but which in Israel are still very much alive.

I cannot pretend to include here even a small proportion of the many things that have influenced Israel during its first forty years. I once read an item which stunned me: Israel is the third most prolific source of news stories in the world after the United States and the Soviet Union. If we could find a way of selling news about ourselves our budgetary problems would be solved overnight! It is impossible to try to summarize even the most important events. Instead, I shall attempt to sketch a model, schematic and arbitrary as all models are but one at least that provides a rudimentary guide to forty turbulent years which to the distant observer may seem an amorphous mass of repetitive and dramatic conflict.

My model divides Israel's first forty years into two periods of approximately equal length and of markedly different character. I believe that nobody will dispute this division. The line of separation, the great watershed, is clearly the date of 5 June 1967, the start of the Six Day War.

1947/8–1967: The struggle for the very creation and survival of the state.

1967–1988: The struggle for peace and the legitimation of Israel in the Middle Eastern region.

My model then divides, perhaps with artificial symmetry, the first and second periods into eight subperiods:

1947/8–1949: The War of Independence. Birth.

1950–1956: Rapid growth.

1956–1963: Integration and introversion.

1963–1967: Struggle over new leadership.

1967–1973: The war between two wars.

1973–1977: Inner upheaval.

1977–1984: A new regime and major conflicts.

1984–1988: Apparent unity but real divisions.

1947/8–1949 This period marks the difficult, bloody birth of the young state, the most dangerous and critical years. Following the Declaration of the United Nations Assembly on 29 November 1947, which partitioned Palestine into separate Arab and Jewish states, seven Arab countries declared openly and solemnly that they would thwart its implementation with their blood. Israel did indeed come dangerously close to stillbirth and extinction. Between November 1947 and May 1948 (when the State of Israel was officially declared), a total embargo was imposed on the importation of arms into the country. Many states (including the United States) which had supported the UN Declaration began to express serious doubts about the practicability of its implementation. Even a number of Jewish leaders in Israel and in the Diaspora advised postponing any Declaration of Independence. If it had not been for the determination of others – foremost among them David Ben-Gurion, who later served as temporary Prime Minister – a postponement might well have been fatal, and the great opportunity lost.

The War of Independence was literally a battle for life and death. It differed from all the subsequent wars in range, depth, duration and most of all in the deployment of combat forces. The war lasted twenty months and affected every settlement in the country as irregular and untrained Jewish units with only light and a few medium weapons at their disposal stood against whole armies equipped with air power, artillery and armour. The Egyptian army advanced to within 18 miles of Tel Aviv and the Jewish sector of Jerusalem was besieged for weeks on end. The Iraqi and Jordanian armies almost cut the country in two on the narrow coastal plain; in the north the Syrian army penetrated deep into Galilee and the Jordan Valley. If the young state had been defeated in May or June 1948, it is doubtful that anyone would have come to its aid, and the tragedy would have been soon forgotten like so many other tragedies the world has passed by over the last fifty years.

The whole burden of this harsh war was laid on the shoulders of thirty thousand fighters, including paramilitaries and a thousand women. They fought with a courage and initiative unequalled in any of Israel's subsequent wars. Sections operated like battalions and platoons like brigades. Six thousand were killed (1 per cent of the population), many thousands were wounded and taken prisoner, settlements were overrun and destroyed. Even when cease-fire agreements were signed with the four states bordering Israel – Egypt, Jordan, Lebanon and Syria – in mid 1949, following the outstanding Israeli victory, everyone knew deep down that they would never lead to peace. This was just a lull before the next round.

1950–1956 The next period is marked by the second courageous decision of the leadership, headed by Ben-Gurion: to open up the land without restriction to mighty waves of immigration that would *treble* the existing population. (This would be the equivalent, for example, of Britain, with its fifty or so million inhabitants, absorbing a hundred million new residents in just six years). Such a dramatic and prodigious growth in population demanded a regime of firm economic austerity: for hundreds of thousands of immigrants, arrival in the Promised Land meant consignment to crowded transit camps and severe hardship. The host community, which had become accustomed to its own ways in the twenty years prior to the establishment of the state, suffered its own identity crisis. All this took place while new democratic institutions were being built and against a background of constant anxiety about the country's military preparedness against the threat from without. Security preoccupations grew in intensity until the Suez operation of the mid 1950s, which effectively postponed the next round for another ten years and so gave Israel the chance to consolidate and prepare itself for the inevitable onslaught.

1956–1963 The third period was perhaps the most introverted in all the years of Israel's existence. This was its adolescent period, when all energy was directed inwards towards the development of its personality. It was a time when building and growth were *not* spurred by external circumstances such as massive immigration. Relative international peace, quiet borders and the dormant condition of the Arab-Israeli dispute enabled Israel to engage in a vigorous programme of construction and development. The Israeli identity began to emerge and crystallize, and the trial of Adolf Eichmann was a first step in the process of exorcizing the trauma of the Holocaust. Israel also began to broaden its links with the newly independent states of Africa and Asia; this little country, an infant in the international arena, saw itself able and even obliged to provide special aid to other countries. The easing of tension also encouraged the revival of political ambitions, and the first signs of dissension within the leadership appeared.

The period ends in 1963 with the final departure from public life of David Ben-Gurion, the leader and father-figure, the "old man" as he was called even when he was far from old in the biological sense. He was a charismatic figure, a democratic socialist of supreme political and moral authority, a blend of Lenin, Nehru and Churchill. He was an exceptional figure in Jewish history, which during the centuries of the Diaspora produced few leaders of real stature.

1963–1967 From 1963 to 1967 there was a slight stirring of the dormant Arab-Israeli dispute, with controversy over the exploitation of water sources in the north, the founding of the Palestine Liberation Organization and the growth of international tensions in Vietnam, Cuba and Greece. In Israel intercommunal rivalry began to emerge, and the higher echelons of government, lacking Ben-Gurion's guiding hand, were plunged into wrangling between bureaucratic socialism and more centralist liberal-nationalist policies. The period was brought to an abrupt end by the Six Day War which fell upon Israel suddenly, rousing the dormant dispute with the Arab world and fanning into flame at a single stroke what had smouldered quietly for years.

This marks the beginning of the second half.

1967–1973 The years between the end of the Six Day War and the outbreak of the Yom Kippur War (October 1973) were marked by strong and conflicting emotions: relief at the removal of the burden of dread which had oppressed Israeli society on the eve of the Six Day War, but disappointment that peace had not been achieved and had, in fact, become even more problematic and remote. There was a widespread feeling that Israel had been born anew, as if the previous birth in 1948 had been only partial and was now completed, but this new and powerful awareness began to unnerve the world and even some citizens of the state. Emotions were aroused on the one hand by the severance of relations with the Eastern bloc, the bitter hostility of the Third World which hitherto had appeared for the most part amicable, and the severe criticism from left-wing circles in the West which had always been supportive of Israel; and on the other hand, by the forging of close and warm relations with the Jews of the Diaspora and the receipt of unprecedented support and aid from the United States.

The new reality created by the war was not confined to the corridors of politics and diplomacy, however. It was a vivid and sometimes painful fact confronting every Israeli. The Palestinian problem was no longer the stuff of newspaper articles: it was now a reality made concrete in the form of a population (one-third of the total Israeli population) under Israeli administration. In addition, the pace of terrorism accelerated and the War of Attrition, as it came to be called, led to a renewal of fighting on the cease-fire lines of the Canal Zone.

Many imagine the years between the two great wars to be a time of peace and tranquility when Israelis rested on their laurels. This is possibly true of one or two years preceding the Yom Kippur War, but most of the period was spent wrestling with new and complex internal problems and in facing up to the War of Attrition, which dragged on from day to day with no end in sight. The President of Egypt, Gamal Abdel Nasser, who led the Arab rejectionist front at the postwar Khartoum Conference (no peace, no negotiation, no recognition) said something very true: "If we succeed in causing Israel not an average of one killed per day but an average of five or six, then we shall be setting out on the road to victory." His wish was very nearly fulfilled. It was only through military and political initiatives, which made the war more painful to the Egyptians than to the Israelis (in spite of the Egyptians' vastly superior reserves of population and territory), that Israel succeeded in persuading Egypt to agree to a renewed cease-fire. Peace of a kind lasted a few short years until the outbreak of the Yom Kippur War, which Arab intransigence and Israeli complacency made inevitable.

The Yom Kippur War created a deep trauma, not only because of its suddenness but because it forced a complete re-evaluation of the myth of absolute military superiority which many Israelis had taken for granted since 1967, a myth nourished by reams of heroic anecdotes and triumphalism. Yet in spite of this, in spite of the initial shock and the reversals of the first days, the war produced a military victory no less impressive than that of 1967. In the Six Day War Israel was like a well-prepared student who has passed an exam with a high grade. In the Yom Kippur War Israel was like the same student who has not opened a book or attended a lecture for weeks, and when the exam is suddenly sprung upon him he buckles down and writes in haste and manages to score a good, or at least an above-average, mark. Experienced teachers would place a higher value on the latter performance.

But such excuses did nothing to reassure the nation, now experiencing a crisis of confidence in its leadership fuelled by Left and Right in equal part. Everyone felt at the end of the war that a new era was beginning.

1973–1977 Israeli society begins to polarize. Thirst for peace on the one hand and doubts about its likelihood on the other create serious political tension. Israel is no longer "waiting for a phone call from the Arabs", as Moshe Dayan arrogantly remarked after the Six Day War. Loss of faith in the leadership and anger at the cost of the war united the public in a longing for change which found expression in the elections of 1977. The Labour Party, which had been in power for twenty-nine years (as well as for many years before 1948 in the institutions of the "state in the making"), suffered a crushing defeat and new forces, a different ruling culture, were thrust centre-stage. The veteran opposition leader, Menachem Begin, who had been unsuccessfully challenging Ben-Gurion's authority since the first Knesset in 1949, finally succeeded after the old man's death in trouncing his contentious and discredited heirs.

1977–1984 The seventh period is marked by upheavals of mind-boggling intensity. It was as if the opposition, which had long been thought incapable of winning an election, sought to achieve at once everything that had been denied it over the years. The new right-wing regime needed to establish its legitimacy as a matter of urgency, and to prove itself not merely as a substitute for a failed administration but as worthy in its own right. All at once different and contradictory initiatives were unleashed, first and foremost among them being the Camp David accords of 1979 bringing peace with Egypt and withdrawal from the whole of Sinai. On the other hand, however, there was massive colonization of the West Bank, rash economic measures and bitter conflict with the new opposition which had yet to come to terms with its loss of power. This was a period of polemic and strife and huge demonstrations, and an election campaign in 1981 fraught with tension and laced with venom. The government tried to consolidate itself with the war in Lebanon, begun in June 1982, but this only drove the population into a state of absolute polarization until the 1984 elections, which produced utter stalemate. It became clear that two options were available: either internecine strife to the bitter end or some form of bipartisan government to prevent a slide into real civil war. The outcome was the establishment of the Government of National Unity.

1984–1988 This cannot be called a time of real national unity. Rather it is a time of national reconciliation and temporary calm before the storm. The basic agenda is to repair the damage of recent years – withdrawal from Lebanon and economic stabilization – but the central problem, the question of ceding the Occupied Territories, has been frozen until the elections due in 1988. Few observers expect any significant electoral change, so stalemate is likely to continue. The nation had been unsettled enough in the early 1980s actually to prefer stalemate and apparent national unity to a new series of political storms.

This essay is being written at a time of dramatically increased tension in Israel, and what the coming months and years will bring is still an unknown quantity. Yet I have taken the risk of including 1988 in the last period of my model not simply to round up the years to a symmetrical forty (1948–1988). I honestly believe that *now* is the time to conclude peace with Jordan, the Palestinians and Syria. All the factors on the ground favour this, all the foundations are solid, and it is better that peace be made under the aegis of the Government of National Unity than by the slender majority of one party or another.

The Arab-Israeli dispute is already more than a century old, dating back to the early 1880s when the first Zionists arrived in Greater Israel. No international dispute has engaged the world's attention for so long. Nothing more needs to happen for peace to be achieved. There is no need for another war or a revival of terrorist activity or an oil crisis or a new international dispute; even détente between the great powers is unnecessary. All that is needed between the two peoples is a recognition *in the heart* (I believe that intellectual recognition already exists) that the Palestinians cannot destroy Israel, nor Israel the Palestinians.

CHAPTER TWO

THE PEOPLE

Half the people of the world
Loves the other half
Half the people of the world
Hates the other half.

Is it because of one or the other
That I must wander and change without cease?

YEHUDA AMIHAI

Four million three hundred thousand Israeli citizens are listed in alphabetical innocence in the pages of the register of population, every one of them concealing ancestries that reach out to the corners of the world. Behind them are different religions, different cultures and different languages. The Israeli melting pot and the marvellous stories that form its ingredients are often taken for granted, but will it ever amount to a national identity?

I believe that the last forty years have indeed clothed every Israeli in a new and quite recognizable identity, a subtle blend of landscape, light, custom, diet and language. How deep this identity is and how stable is not yet clear, but it exists, and in many senses it is more intense and fundamental that the identity of the American in 1816, forty years after the Declaration of Independence. It is not my intention here to map the roots of national identity, or to tease apart the myriad tiny hints which indicate its presence. I am concerned rather with its leaves and branches, with what is explicit, with divisions and conflicting dreams. I want to sketch in large and general lines some of the contours of Israeli society.

The most immediate division, and it dominates political debate, is that between the advocates of Greater Israel, meaning all of western Palestine, and those who favour partition in the form of a Palestinian or Jordanian-Palestinian state and withdrawal from the Occupied Territories. Geographically, the division could not be more clear. On the one side are those who want Israel to continue to occupy the West Bank and the Gaza Strip which were captured during the Six Day War, or simply to annex them, thereby adding 2229 square miles, nearly one-third of the State's original area. Support for the policy ranges from those who would grant full citizenship to all the one and a quarter million Palestinians in the territories, through those who would prefer to leave them as foreign nationals with Jordanian passports or refugee status, to a hard core who intend to expel them by persuasion or force. Their opponents support the restoration of the whole of the West Bank and Gaza, or significant portions of them, to Jordan or to the Palestinians themselves, subject to demilitarization and security guarantees. For some it is a matter of demographic considerations and a desire to preserve the Jewish character of the state. Others argue from a wish to encourage the peace process or a moral recognition of the Palestinians' right to self-determination.

This is the sharpest line of latitude dividing Israeli society and the political map, between "hawks" and "doves", though it is in constant flux. It colours almost everything and careful study of a speaker's tail feathers for signs of dovish white or hawkish grey will indicate his position on virtually any other issue.

An entirely different line divides the religious and the secular: those who interpret their Jewishness as a national attribute and see their religious heritage merely as a part of their culture – just as a secular Frenchman sees Christianity as part of his cultural heritage – from those who call themselves religious and see the kernel of their Jewish identity as inseparable from the religious faith of Israel. The religious view the state only as the first stage in their dream that the Rabbinical Law should eventually constitute the legislature of Israel. Secularists consider religion a private matter entirely separate from the state. They also believe the forces of religious tradition to be in retreat and certainly unfit either to administer a modern state or to direct Israeli culture.

The division between religious and secular is of great significance. Its foundations are solid and it arouses heated arguments over the conduct of daily life. Orthodox and other believers wish to impose religious norms not only on the rules of traditional observance such as *kashruth* (dietary law), the Sabbath and festivals, but also in personal matters such as marriage, divorce and burial. The secular camp has usually managed to resist their calls or at least water them down, but success depends on the political constellation of the day in the Knesset where religious parties control only about 15 per cent of the vote but are adept at wringing concessions from the major parties.

The secular camp is often seen as a diffuse coalition compared with the religious monolith, but in fact both sides are equally divided. Religious sects abound, the more extreme vehemently denying the very legitimacy of the state. They would rather be ruled by King Hussein or Yasser Arafat than by "apostate" Jews who deny the authority of Rabbinical Law, which has little time for modern notions of democracy and consensus. Members of these sects are sometimes called "Black" Jews because they only wear black, and indeed the more uncompromising among them adopt the Central European dress of several centuries ago: black hat, gown and stockings. Much has been said and written about them and the self-imposed ghettos in which they live cut off from the modern world. They do not serve in the army, they have no radios or television sets and they read only religious newspapers.

Secular society usually treats "Black" Jews with a mixture of scorn, contempt, pity, hatred, respect and admiration, sometimes fear as well. They are not greatly loved but few Israelis, if seriously pressed, believe the country would be better off without them providing they keep themselves to themselves and do not incite religious controversy. They are often far from easy to approach, covering their faces with their hats and fleeing at the first sign of an inquisitive journalist or photographer, or sometimes even attacking them. (From his photographs it is clear that Frédéric Brenner is expert in catching such elusive prey, and in winning their trust and gaining access to the sanctum of their prayer schools. His image on page 96 is remarkable; taking a camera into the heart of a nuclear reactor is the only fitting analogy.)

"Black" Jews are few in number and confined to particular parts of the country, but they symbolize some fundamental core of Jewish identity, metaphysical but also real. They symbolize, too, all the absurdities and paradoxes of Jewish existence. Dressed like Polish aristocrats from the sixteenth century, they represent a Jewish clock which has stopped, but they are awesomely tenacious in their way of life.

These splinter groups are only a small minority, however, and distinct from them are the majority of religious Jews who recognize the State of Israel but see it as a necessary evil to be used but not to be identified with. Even they, however, see the state as no more than the precursor of divine redemption and all of them combine nationalism with religiosity of Messianic fervour. The soil of Greater Israel is sacred in their Zionist eyes, not only as a national interest but as a metaphysical concept. The most fervent among them even dream of rebuilding the Temple.

The national-religious debate is the deepest debate in the history of the Jewish people; three thousand years have not for a moment blunted its importance. To think that such a struggle could be resolved by the legal-political establishment of a modern state is an illusion; on the contrary, it will nourish Jewish and hence Israeli identity until its last day. It may provoke conflict, but it remains a fertile catalyst which forces the secular nationalist Jew to confront his beliefs, or lack of them, no less than it forces the religious Jew to emerge from the cocoon of Rabbinical Law and expose himself to the practical realities of a modern state.

A third and no less crucial line in Israeli society is that between Jews and Palestinians, whether Christian or Muslim. Minorities such as the Druse and Circassians stand between them. This is the line which separates the 82 per cent of Jews and the 18 per cent of Palestinians within the Israel of the Green Line (the pre-1967 borders) or the 62.5 per cent of Jews and the 37.5 per cent of Palestinians in the Greater Israel combining the Occupied Territories. Although this issue is often oversimplified, few Israelis would deny that it splits the country like no other: a fundamental and deeply bitter dispute between two peoples claiming rights to the same land and beside which other ideological schisms pale into relative insignificance.

Even those who appreciate the dispute's overriding importance, however, cannot afford to ignore the shades of opinion among Palestinians, even inside the Green Line. Some see Israeli citizenship as something forced upon them and they intend to throw it off at the first opportunity. In the meantime they wish only to consolidate their identity as an autonomous ethnic minority. Others, and their number has increased in recent years, wish to deepen their involvement in the Jewish state and to transform their Israeli citizenship into an identification with Israel. They want their voice to be heard and respected in public discussion, and without going so far as to advocate total assimilation they believe that the Israeli *nation* (whether inside the Green Line or not) will be forced to recognize that it is composed of both Jews and Palestinians who must forge a new identity together.

It is also possible to divide Israeli society not by political or religious or secular values but by cultural origin. This is the long-established division between Western and Oriental, between Ashkenazi Jews, whose origin is mainly in Eastern, Central and Western Europe, and Oriental Jews from Asia, Arabia, North Africa and the southern Mediterranean basin (who include within their number Sephardi Jews of Spanish, Portuguese or North African descent). The difference between them is generalized, because each community is far from homogeneous and can be divided into distinct subgroups. There is little in common between Anglo-Saxon and Rumanian Jews, for example, although they both belong to the Ashkenazi community, and there are profound differences between Jews from Bulgaria and Yemen, although formally both groups are Oriental.

Before the Holocaust, Ashkenazim made up 91 per cent of world Jewry, and even after the extermination of whole national communities during the Second World War they still remain the majority today. In Israel, however, they are now outnumbered by Oriental Jews who account for more than half the Jewish population. Oriental Jews generally occupy the lower rungs of society and many still remember the severe hardships of settling in the country in the early 1950s. This inevitably sets up cultural and economic tensions which swell and ebb according to a logic of their own. In recent years they have surfaced in acrimonious debates about whether Israel's identity lies in a Western or an Oriental future. Though in practice conflict is assuaged by a degree of intermarriage between the two communities, such marriages still affect only 20 per cent of the population and are mainly confined to wealthier families. A certain amount of tolerance and plugging of economic gaps has reduced the traditional rivalry between Oriental Jews and Ashkenazim, but many Israelis continue to view the Arab-Israeli conflict as a diversion from the real conflict between East and West. When peace eventually comes, the latter will preoccupy the country much more than it does today.

Yet another line in the strata, however, bisects and to some extent neutralizes this potentially serious divide. This line is between those who were born in Israel and those who were not. Careful observers of the immigrant community make a further distinction between those who came to Israel of their own free will, a minority, and those who had no choice but to come. The second category comprises German Jews who fled to Israel in the early 1930s, for example, survivors of the Holocaust who left a shattered Europe in the late 1940s and Iraqi Jews who were driven here soon after the state was created. The first includes Russian Jews from the waves of immigration in the first decades of the century, and again in recent years, and Jews from Morocco, Yemen and the United States.

Three decades ago the line was very prominent indeed, though it has faded over the years. Since Independence, Israel has received nearly 1,800,000 immigrants from 70 different countries; in contrast some 350,000 people have left. It is home to 27.4 per cent of world Jewry, as opposed to only 6.36 per cent in 1948, and 61 per cent of its citizens are native-born instead of only 35 per cent at Independence. The ratio is still significant enough to be important to an understanding of Israeli society.

Such divisions, such fault lines in the social strata, might suggest a rather gloomy society riven by internal contradictions, wavering between different identities, a society which bears within itself the memory of incongruous cultural roots transplanted from all the ends of the earth. One must remember, too, that as recently as 1984–5 Israel absorbed the Ethiopian Jewish community, a dislocating experience for many thousands of people who had to jump from an isolated, famine-struck existence to Western civilization all at once. What indeed is there in common between a devout Muslim who sympathizes with the policies of Ayatollah Khomeini and an Orthodox nationalist who would like to demolish the Dome of the Rock, rebuild the Temple and restore the House of David? What common ground can there possibly be between a black-clad Hasid from Eastern Europe, with his fur hat and stockings, and a left-wing kibbutznik who likes rock music and favours a secular state?

For all its manifest internal contradictions, however, the truth is that Israeli society has generally remained democratic and responsible, not only since the state was founded but in the many decades of "the state in the making" when the Jewish community had no national independence worth the name. Wars of liberation almost always end in power struggles, but the level of violence in Israeli society was minimal both before the state was established and, especially, afterwards. In a century of Zionism perhaps thirty or forty Jews have been killed by other Jews for ideological or political reasons. Perhaps half a dozen have died since 1948, years which have seen turbulent difficulties of every complexion. One man, I think, was murdered for political motives in settlement of a score dating back to the Holocaust, and a religious activist was fatally injured in a confrontation with the police during a demonstration over the Sabbath. I do not recall a single case of a politician being murdered for his opinions, and political extremes in Israel are far apart indeed.

The last person to die in such circumstances fell in 1982 at the height of the acrimony over the war in Lebanon. After the publication of the Kahan Commission's report on the massacre carried out by Lebanese Christians in the Palestinian refugee camps of Sabra and Chatila, in which the Israeli army was implicated by its reluctance to intervene, members of the Peace Now movement took part in a vigorous demonstration against the Begin government. They demanded the dismissal of the Minister of Defence, Ariel Sharon. Government supporters organized a counter demonstration nearby, one of them throwing a grenade into the crowd of Peace Now activists which injured several people and killed Emil Grunzweig, a young researcher at the Van Leer Institute in Jerusalem. His death shocked the entire nation, and both Left and Right joined together in planting a memorial grove where he fell near the Prime Minister's office. It came as no surprise, and I would say it was almost inevitable, that Menachem Begin himself, the Prime Minister against whom Emil Grunzweig had demonstrated so vociferously, led the dedication ceremony.

Sometimes, paradoxically, it is the very existence of so many cracks and rifts which prevents the formation of two extremes so violently opposed that civil war would become a serious possibility. We all live many lives, for temporary alliances between those who otherwise have little in common are a necessary virtue of social life. So, for example, a committed left-winger, secular and a "dove", who is passionately against right-wing solutions to the Palestinian problem, will stand shoulder to shoulder with ideological enemies in a demonstration against the closing of cinemas in Jerusalem on Sabbath Eve. On the other side of the police cordon will be the religious faction, many wearing their yarmulkes (the Jewish skullcap), its ranks made up of nationalists who believe passionately in Greater Israel, and see the present state as only the beginning of redemption, and "Black" Jews who never celebrate Independence Day and will allow no national flags or other symbols in their schools.

Or, again, a member of the extreme *Shomer Ha-tzair* (the Young Guard kibbutz movement), a hard-line socialist, will find himself beside a religious nationalist of the *Gush Emunim* party, whose views on every subject are diametrically opposed to his, in a demonstration outside the Finnish Embassy (which represents Soviet interests) demanding that Russian Jews be allowed to emigrate. A young intellectual, a right-wing Sephardi, will pass them by with indifference and even hostility, fearful lest an influx of Jewish intellectuals from the USSR should jeopardize his hard-won social status after years of struggling to escape from his humble origins.

Palestinians will demonstrate with Jews against racism and for peace, and they will be confronted by Druse policemen from elite units of the border guard who are not renowned for their tolerance. All these lives, these temporary alliances and shards of identity, flex and reassemble like the image in a kaleidoscope. What appears from a distance to be a struggle between extremes is, on closer analysis, a mirage. Israel's seemingly polarized society is just a society searching for its national, territorial and social identity.

The real divisions in Israeli society, therefore, are between those who accept the state as a given fact, as a necessary and natural bureaucratic system, and who will meet their obligations as citizens providing they receive appropriate services in return, and those for whom the state is still conditional, to be acknowledged only in so far as it helps to realize a social, national or religious aspiration. The first Zionists said to themselves: if we have come this far in order to establish a national home, if we are here to create something out of nothing, there is no point in recreating the states we have left behind. We have the chance to open a new page, for in our hearts we have the blueprint of a new society. Our brothers in Europe are fighting to change institutions entrenched over centuries; we who have no institutions can build them properly from the start.

Pragmatists don't change the world; prophets do. After forty years the country's institutions are now firmly established and the ranks of the ideological vanguard are thinning, but their voice still calls insistently in the land as if all the world were still possible. Pragmatists, those cool engineers of consensus, are very good at solutions but rarely dare to break any moulds. The ultimate dividing line in Israeli society is between those who can adjust to a *status quo* and those who believe Israel to be only the beginning of a great opportunity, that four decades are merely the first sentence in the long and complex text they are destined to write.

CHAPTER THREE

THE LAND

Dress me, good mother, in a coat of many colours
And lead me at dawn to my labour.
My land is swathed in light like a prayer shawl,
Houses stand forth like frontlets,
And the roads paved by hand stream down like the straps of philactories.

AVRAHAM SHLONSKY

Main routes
Other routes
0 10 20 30 40 Kilometres
0 5 10 15 20 25 Miles
Mediterranean Sea
LEBANON
SYRIA
GOLAN
GALILEE
SAMARIA
JUDAEA
JORDAN
MOAB
Mt Hermon
Dan
Kiryat Shemona
El Quneitra
Rosh Hanikra
Bar'am
Rihaniya
Hula Valley
Nahariyya
Jatt
Meron
Hazor
Safed
Jordan
Qasrin
Mt Peres
Akko (Acre)
Yam Kinneret (Sea of Galilee)
HAIFA
Tiberias
En Gev
Yarmuk
Mt Carmel
Atlit
Bet Shearim
Nazareth
Mt Tabor
Jezreel Valley
Afula
Zikhron Ya'akov
Megiddo
Caesarea
Bet Shean
Jenin
Hadera
Netanya
Tulkarm
Nablus
Herzliyya
TEL AVIV-YAFO (Jaffa)
Petah Tiqwa
Rishon Le Ziyyon
Lod
Ramla
Rehovot
Ramallah
Jericho
Allenby Bridge
Wadi Qilt
AMMAN
Mevasseret Ziyyon
JERUSALEM
Abu Gosh
Ashdod
Qumran
Bethlehem
Mar Saba
Ashqelon
Kiryat Gat
Bet Guvrin
Mizpe Shalem
Dead Sea
Hebron
GAZA

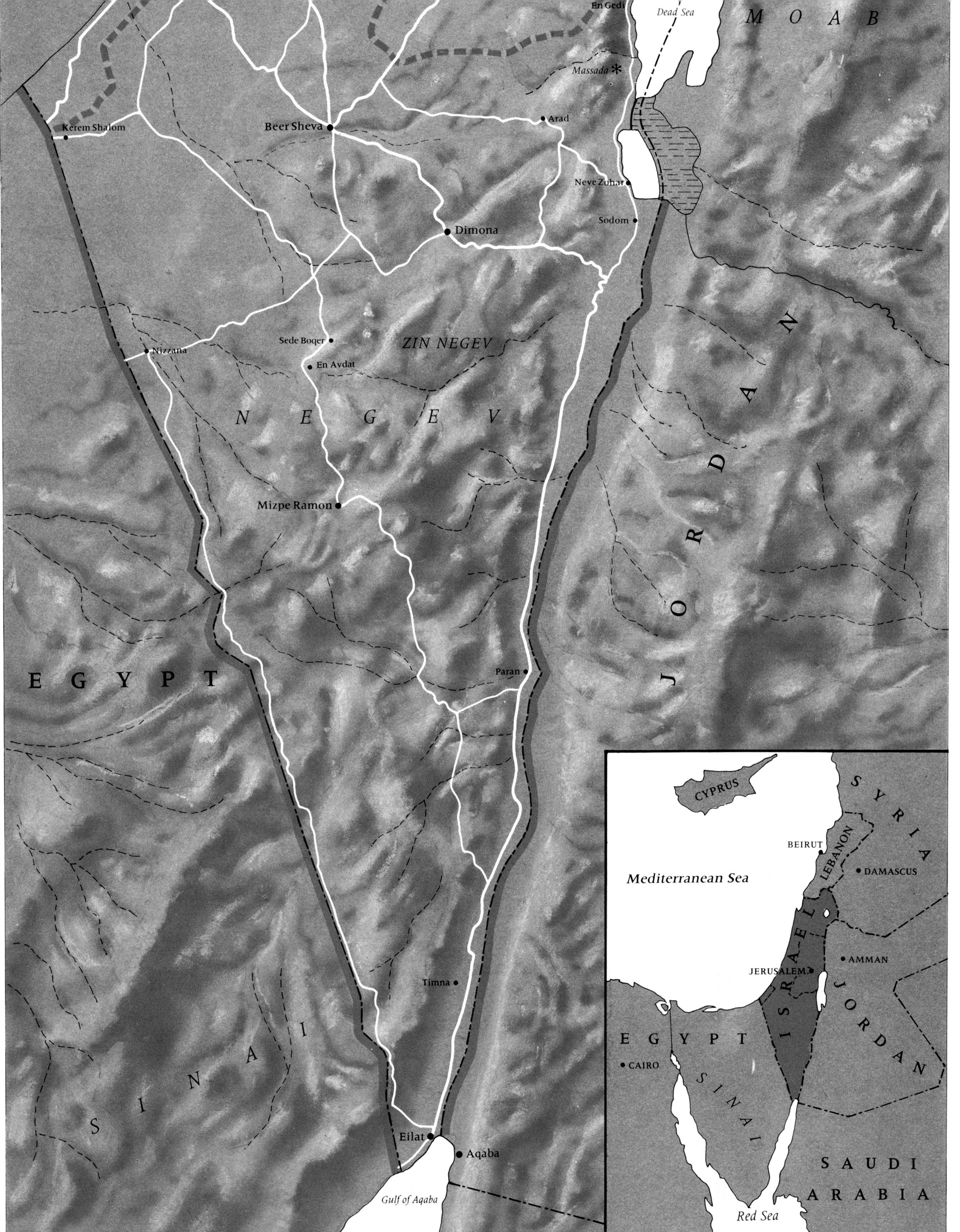
En Gedi
Dead Sea
M O A B
Massada
Kerem Shalom
Beer Sheva
Arad
Neve Zohar
Sodom
Dimona
Sede Boqer
ZIN NEGEV
Nizzana
En Avdat
N E G E V
J O R D A N
Mizpe Ramon
E G Y P T
Paran
Timna
S I N A I
Eilat
Aqaba
Gulf of Aqaba
CYPRUS
S Y R I A
BEIRUT
LEBANON
DAMASCUS
Mediterranean Sea
AMMAN
JERUSALEM
ISRAEL
E G Y P T
JORDAN
CAIRO
SINAI
S A U D I
A R A B I A
Red Sea

Israel is not the only country in the world which a good driver with a trustworthy car can circumnavigate in one day. Nor is it the only country with magnificent scenery and a variety of climates: sea and desert, snow and plain. But Israel is one of the very few places where a day's drive will take in not only startlingly varied scenery but all four corners of the state as well. There is something significant, compelling even, in finding so much packed into so small an area – only 7993 square miles inside the pre-1967 borders and 444 on the Golan Heights. Landscape affects people profoundly, whether they wish it or not. Nowhere is this more true than the country of my birth.

In this chapter I am going to take you on a day's journey to the four corners of Israel within its present borders. As Frédéric Brenner's beautiful landscape photographs testify, the State of Israel is far from mature. There are many stretches of virgin land; there is much to be done. Most important of all there is room for many more people to settle here, if only they would decide to.

It is a drive I have made a few times before in my life and the prospect of doing so again greatly appeals. I do not plan to visit the 2229 square miles of the West Bank and Gaza Strip, nor of course the 23,500 square miles of Sinai that were returned to Egypt several years ago. I will pause from time to time to call attention to the physical and human landscapes captured in Frédéric Brenner's photographs. He is a Frenchman who has made a career of photographing the steadily diminishing Jewish communities in remote areas all over the world such as Yemen, Ethiopia, North Africa, Soviet Central Asia and India. The idea for this book is his, and he sees it as a kind of dialogue between the Israeli Jew and the Jew living in the Diaspora, the Jew photographing and the Israeli writing. The essential dialogue is for the reader to discover in the interplay of pictures and text. But as I believe the final right of reply belongs to the written word, I have included here some personal impressions of his art.

05.00 Haifa

Time to leave my house on one of the western spurs of the Carmel in Haifa, Israel's northern port. A quiet spring dawn, plants everywhere in flower and the lush vegetation, after a winter of plentiful rain, has yet to be burnished by the sun. Far below through my window a thin vapour lies on the Mediterranean and out on the water, still grey at this early hour, the passenger ferry from Greece is just coming into view. The Mount Carmel range is not high, averaging about 1000 feet, but its western side rises almost sheer out of the water and from its peaks there are panoramic views of the great bay curving north, past the town of Akko, to the white cliff of Rosh Hanikra, the border between Israel and Lebanon some 25 miles away.

The descent from the Carmel at this hour of the morning is fast and within just a few minutes I am passing north through Israel's heavy industrial sector: refineries and petrochemical plants, engineering shops and cement factories which work through the night. A cloud of toxic dust from their chimneys still clings at this dawn hour to the mountainside and colours it purple. These are Haifa's old northern suburbs which in recent years have become independent townships, jealously guarding their new-found autonomy. Although the shoreline is barely a mile or two to my left there is no sign of the sea, just the emphatic flatness of the land with its tangle of shops, houses and small businesses.

A few minutes later the urban sprawl thins to reveal the sea once more, now flickering behind the high fences of the giant Tactical Research Authority complex, where hundreds of Israel's best scientists are engaged in defence and weapons research. Some of Israel's most closely guarded secrets are concealed behind those fences. It is now some thirty minutes since I left the Carmel and I am on a fast, two-lane highway joining trucks and the first delivery vans speeding towards the distinctive profile of Akko, the old Crusader fort of St Jean d'Acre, dividing the bay and jutting out into the sea, with its picturesque harbour, palm trees and stately minarets. In the beautifully preserved old town there are many mosques and Arab caravanserais. The sea is quite choppy at this time of year and the air is cool, although it already contains a hint of the summer heat which will come upon us all too soon.

The highway, now busy with traffic, skirts east of the town and is fringed with the stalls of Arab traders, full of big clay pots, colourful wicker baskets and the ubiquitous piles of fruit and vegetables. The scene reminds me of Frédéric Brenner's photograph on page 117, but this view is liable to mislead: in recent years a significant proportion of the Arab population has worked hard to achieve a more sophisticated and professional life style. I am thinking, for example, of some of the Arab students I have taught over the past twenty years. I remember one from a small and remote village in the hills of Galilee, his Hebrew far from fluent, who applied himself so assiduously to the study of comparative literature that within a few years he was able to write an excellent dissertation on the "stream of consciousness" technique in the novels of Virginia Woolf and wrestle with the most demanding English critical works. I am thinking of an Arab actor in the Municipal Theatre of Haifa who has played many leading roles and won the Israel Prize, or of my Arab friend Anton Shammas, author of *Arabesques*. He writes in Hebrew, mastering the language as Nabokov and Conrad mastered English.

It is not all smooth, however. Sometimes even the most formidably well-educated Arabs are the focus of acrimonious talk about national rights and the conceptual basis of Zionism. Jews sometimes accuse them of enjoying the fruits of Israeli democracy while subverting the fabric of national life, but their success is a proof of the vitality and openness of the Jewish society in which they live.

From Akko the highway leads between orchards and fields to Nahariyya, which was founded more than fifty years ago by immigrants from Germany.

Glancing at the beach I can see tanned and white-haired Teutonic gentlemen performing their calisthenic exercises. By coming here they may have missed some good Wagnerian concerts at Bayreuth, but they have gained a Jewish life and warm water close to their homes of which their erstwhile fellow countrymen, shivering in the chill of the North Sea, can only dream. On the right stands the immense aqueduct built by the Turks, now a lonely backdrop to the nearby kibbutz of Lohamei Hageta'ot, founded in 1949 by survivors from Nazi concentration camps. On 19 April each year, they commemorate the anniversary of the Warsaw Uprising.

Frédéric Brenner has skilfully captured an instant in another Israeli ritual of great power which is now a vital element of Israel's brief tradition (pages 2–3). On the morning of Israel's two official remembrance days – Holocaust Memorial Day and the Day of Remembrance for the fallen in Israel's wars – sirens all over the country signal two minutes' silence during which all work stops, all traffic comes to a standstill and people come together in memory of the dead.

When a brief silence first became a part of the ceremony, soon after the state was founded, few people took much notice. It was thought too formal and impersonal, but sometimes we can watch simple rituals gather strength until they become inseparable from the fabric of tradition. Gradually, as if by some unspoken national agreement, the idea took hold and more and more people joined in this act of respect. In a country of many voices, often loud and angry, silence is catharsis. People stand motionless in shops; cars halt on the streets; many people just stand quietly at home, unseen but still honouring the memory of the dead.

I cannot speak on anyone's behalf, least of all the dead. Yet I dare to think that those millions who died alone in a foreign land would be pleased to know that fifty, sixty, a hundred years after their dreadful deaths, their brothers and their new fellow countrymen pause from their work, here in the ancient homeland, and stand in silent grief determined above all to remember.

06.00 Rosh Hanikra

Rosh Hanikra, the most northerly point of the coast of Israel, is only a quarter of an hour beyond Nahariyya. When peace finally comes it will be possible to travel on from here to Lebanon, Syria and Turkey; near the border the tracks of the old Cairo–Beirut railway, remains of a more gracious age, are still visible. The light is growing stronger now. Israel is a country of *at once*. Sunrise is brief, sunset is quick and twilight is short-lived; winter and summer change abruptly into one another, and as we shall see the same is true of the scenery.

After an hour in the car my thoughts turn to breakfast, but that is to come. Instead I turn east off the coastal highway and up into the mountains which stand like a high wall between Israel and Lebanon, a natural border. It is an uneven, twisting road and it pays to pause here and look back over Israel's long coastal strip, which is remarkably narrow, only a few miles wide. Most of the country is mountainous, but because people are concentrated in the coastal plain they tend not to think so.

The road follows the border into the heart of western Galilee. This is hardly the Alps but the hills are still quite high, rising to nearly 4000 feet. The vegetation is dense and rich, trees such as the common oak and the native terebinth are planted everywhere. You have to concentrate here, the road rising and falling among villages whose residents have already been up for some time, to judge by the tractors giving way to me on the narrow road and the yellow minibuses ferrying children to school. Farming is adapted to mountain conditions: poultry and cattle, plantations on the foothills. Most of the villages are Jewish, cooperatives and kibbutzim. There are large Arab villages a little farther to the south, on the second tier of western Galilee, though from time to time I pass an Arab or Druse hamlet on the slopes of one of the hills – bare white houses clustered together, a Mediterranean prospect but also very exposed and quite different from the new Jewish settlements.

This part of Galilee is now relatively calm and tranquil, although its few people are used to hardship and danger. Only in recent years has the border been effectively fenced and sealed; before then, settlers had to contend with terrorist incursions and Katyusha rocket attacks. Stretches of the road run right beside the security fence. This morning a half-track is kicking up dust as it rumbles along the unpaved road on the far side, followed by a squad of sappers checking the ground for mines and fresh footprints. Beyond them I can see a Lebanese village, now on scrubland. The woods which originally clothed the area have been cleared for new development.

07.00 The Hula Valley

Three-quarters of an hour later and I am looking out over the Galilee panhandle, or the eastern plain of Upper Galilee, towards the Hula Valley, a short section of the Great Rift Valley which begins near the Syrian–Turkish border, passes through Israel and Jordan to the Red Sea and continues south to East Africa, a relatively narrow but exceptionally long volcanic rift. The Upper Galilee plain is narrow, too – five or six miles wide – and was formerly a gigantic marsh, Lake Hula, which has been drained. Only a small nature reserve retains the original habitat. At seven o'clock in the morning, looking east with the sun on my face, the whole of the valley is spread out before me, rich agricultural land dotted with settlements and scores of sparkling fish ponds.

The descent along the edge of the hills is steep, the road dropping from 2500 feet or so above sea level to only 200 very quickly as it snakes towards Kiryat Shemona, Israel's northern-most town and the constant target in the 1970s and early '80s of the Katyusha rocket attacks which gave moral backing to the controversial war in Lebanon. A few hundred yards along the main street I draw up beside a row of cafés. Breakfast in Israel is often a big meal, with good strong coffee, fruit juice, fresh bread, cheese, olives and salad. That is a little too much for today's schedule – I'll settle for coffee and rolls. This is the floor of the valley, and from where I sit I can see the Hermon range, pink in the morning sun, 10 miles to the northeast.

A quarter of an hour later, restored and refreshed, I'm driving parallel to the Lebanese border past a line of military depots. By them young conscripts stand with their kit bags, hoping for a lift into town. In his photographs, Frédéric Brenner has chosen to show the Israeli army not on parade or with squadrons of aircraft or tanks, but in these very humane pictures of ordinary reservists.

To understand the secret of Israel's military success there is no need to be familiar with the tactics of aerial combat or sophisticated battlefied computers. It is enough to understand the procedures of reserve service, since this is why Israel has been able to field an army of several hundred thousand men against vastly greater Arab armies with almost unlimited manpower. The ability to move smoothly and rapidly from civilian to military life while maintaining a high degree of professionalism is the essence of the nation's military strength. It also guarantees that the army is truly a people's army, one which belongs to all and in which all who wish to can participate.

At the age of eighteen all Jewish and Druse citizens, men and women, are called up for a period of military service (Arabs may serve only if they wish to because there is a profound conflict of loyalties). Thereafter, from the ages of twenty-one to to forty-nine, they are required to return to the army for a few weeks every year to renew their military skills and their familiarity with military hardware. Or as the contemporary Israeli proverb puts it: reservists are regular soldiers who happen to be on leave for eleven months of the year.

The men gathered in the tent in the photograph on page 153 arrived a few hours ago for annual reserve duty. Each has come from a different world. One is sure to be a professor who was attending a scientific congress in Paris or New York just a few days ago. Beside him stands a bank clerk; reclining in the corner is a shopkeeper who has had difficulty finding someone to mind his modest business while he is away. Also present are a student, a farmer, a journalist and one who is unemployed. In short, people of quite different backgrounds and age, family men and bachelors probably of conflicting political opinions. One is religious, another secular; one has left a sick wife at home and another is worried about his exams which he is due to sit in a few weeks. One suffers from high blood pressure and another has rheumatism. Now, for thirty or forty days, they will need to function as one unit, supporting one another during training and on patrol. Their commander, who may be a young man, a student or a kibbutznik, will need tact and common sense to weld all these disparate elements together. He needs to be sensitive to the personalities and particular needs of his platoon (arranging special leave for the student whose exams are imminent, letting the father of seven children spend an extra Sabbath at home), but he must be firm enough to command the respect of his men. Otherwise the whole exercise will be pointless.

I was also pleased with the pictures of young women. The girl with the face of a

Madonna in a crumpled uniform several sizes too big for her (page 103), handling a submachine-gun dripping with black oil and yet still managing to radiate charm and poise, reminds me of the girls in the military bases where I served. Conditions of service were tough and the life was often lonely and fraught with homesickness, but morale was always higher when these young women were with us.

A short distance from the road is the source of the River Jordan and the streams of the Dan, the Banyas and the Shanir which have been left in their wild natural state, with lush vegetation and impressive waterfalls – a moment of welcome tranquility and fortunately too early for tourist coaches. These streams are perhaps the only watercourses in Israel not yet piped or harnessed to pumping stations. The Israeli water authority is an aggressive and efficient body intent on exploiting every drop of water in a country of which more than half, as we shall soon see, is barren desert.

The road now begins to climb and twist on the half-hour ascent to the Hermon range. It is chilly near the summit, a mini-alpine setting at nearly 7000 feet with snow and skiing and a cable car in winter. Today, children and their parents, all well wrapped up, are frolicking in the snow: a pleasant family scene, and as Frédéric Brenner shows elsewhere (pages 180 to 183) family portraits are especially relevant to a study of Israel. They convey social realities, but more significantly they stress the role of the family in the lives of most Israelis. The family in Israel remains a more cohesive and stable institution than in most Western societies. The small size and population of the country encourages firm and enduring family ties; moreover, Israel is a land of immigrants, many of whose families were lost or destroyed during the return to the homeland in the middle years of the century. Those who lost loved ones on their journey here wished only to build the family they no longer had. Close family relationships have always been important to traditional Jewish life. In Israel, no less than in the Diaspora, they are a bulwark against a hostile world.

There is a military observation post up on one of Hermon's peaks (the highest peak is in Syrian hands) from where, if you take the trouble to get a permit in advance, you can look out over the whole of the Lebanon Valley, Israel's coastal strip and even, on a clear day, my home town of Haifa. To the south lies the Kinneret (the Sea of Galilee) and the Jezreel Valley with Mount Tabor in its centre like a brown and perfectly formed breast. This is Israel's most *northerly* point and one of the most breathtaking panoramas in all the Middle East: no wonder one of the soldiers who helped to recapture the observation post after it had fallen to surprise attack in the Yom Kippur War called this place "the eyes of the state". The borders of Israel, Syria and Lebanon converge here, a reminder of how Israel is encircled by the Arab world.

08.00 The Golan Heights

The road forks east on the way down from Hermon and within half an hour I am in the heart of the Golan Heights, a desolate landscape of bare basalt rock rising to nearly 4000 feet and littered with the cones of long-extinct volcanoes. This is frontier country; in the northern sector there are large Druse villages, army camps and UN observation posts, together with a few Jewish settlements which gained a foothold here after the Six Day War. The Golan is a land of grey and black dotted with green, and the general impression, in spite of enclaves of agricultural prosperity, a few gushing streams and some waterfalls, is of aridity, for we are on the edge of the great Syrian desert. The climate is cool and dry.

The Heights are more than 40 miles from north to south and I am now fast approaching Mount Peres, Israel's most *easterly* point, about halfway down. Villages here are few and far between and a lot of military traffic is about: jeeps and trucks roar by me on the road; half-tracks and tanks manoeuvre off it between the occasional minefield. However much I try to ignore them and enjoy the scenery when I'm here, anxiety is never far away. If another war breaks out in the Middle East, this will be where the fighting is fiercest. If peace is concluded with Syria, the border may move a few miles to the west, into Israel, but how far? The Golan Heights are only 12 miles wide from east to west and blood is needlessly shed over the tiniest amounts of territory. Mount Peres, as I pull over while a couple of trucks rush past, looks a little sad and isolated in this exposed landscape.

But now to the south and warmth, for I can see Israel's wonderful lake, the Kinneret, glittering in the sun 1500 feet below the escarpment. Foreigners know this beautiful resort and vast natural reservoir as the Sea of Galilee, but Israelis call it *Yam Kinneret* because in shape it resembles a violin (*kinnor*), although in fact it is more like a viola, and like a violin or viola it arouses the most agreeable thoughts. All around the lake lies the Jordan Valley, fertile and green.

The descent from the Heights is steep, dropping from 1000 feet *above* sea level to more than 600 feet *below* it in only a few minutes. This is where, some eighty years ago, the kibbutz movement was founded – an experiment in life style unique to Israel and still, despite the vicissitudes of time, of modest but solid importance on the country's social map. We can see something of this in Frédéric Brenner's photograph of a kibbutz crèche on page 185. The seven lively toddlers and their three nurses show better than anything from where a kibbutz draws its strength. The crèche, the communal dining hall and members' meetings are its cornerstones. From the look of the room and the tree visible through the window I thought at first this must be one of the long-established and affluent kibbutzim of the Jordan Valley. But it was taken at Mizpe Shalem, on top of a barren hill in the heart of the Judaean Desert not far from the Dead Sea. It is clear that the calm and relaxed atmosphere of this crèche depends neither on where it is nor the amenities it enjoys; rather it emanates from the confidence and composure of the nurses, those stalwart and warm-hearted girls who know how to create a home in the harshest wilderness. Collective and constant investment in children, from the very earliest age, has always been the wellspring of the kibbutz. It breeds a deep sense of assurance in the children and they, in their turn, radiate assurance to the older generation.

The kibbutz as an institution is one of Israel's most impressive shop windows. Not many Israelis are kibbutzniks, perhaps only 2 or 3 per cent of the population, but the way of life is still the focus of much interest. Many hopes are invested in it, there have been not a few disappointments, and expectations are always changing. The strength of the kibbutz movement during the many years of its existence lies in its adaptability. Martin Buber's definition is, I think, the best: the experiment that did not fail. This laconic and modest statement says a great deal. And when we see this crèche in the young kibbutz in the arid hills of Judaea, we appreciate its truth.

But the landscape before me now is a different one. From the Heights, the road curves along the eastern shore of the Kinneret through one of my favourite areas: calm water, the town of Tiberias wrapped in a blue haze on the far side, the scent of earth and banana groves and cotton fields. The land is as fertile as anywhere in southern Europe, though the light is clearer and brighter and in summer the heat is intense. Archaeological evidence tells us that early man lived here many thousands of years ago. He was neither Jew nor Arab nor Christian, just a man by a lake, a fisherman and a hunter.

10.00 Kinneret

The southern end of the lake is only a few miles farther on, right by the Jordanian border and a confluence of rivers, the Jordan emerging from the Kinneret and continuing southwards, and the Yarmuk flowing in from the east. These are not rivers in the Western sense, as they do not reach the sea; rather, in the Middle Eastern sense, they are a source of abundance and life in a barren land. The road heads south along the Great Rift Valley, past prosperous settlements and groves of dates and into the valley of Bet Shean. Here again I can sense the desert in the sandy brown earth. The desert is so characteristic of my country that at times I feel hemmed in by it, but today I am going to avoid it for a few hours and instead turn west towards the valleys of central Israel. Here at last is a real plain, where the Zionist dream was put to the test. Eighty years ago, the whole of this area was covered with festering swamps but the early Jewish pioneers managed to drain the fetid water from its soils and made it land fit for settlement. The next stop is the little town of Afula, which was once seen as the potential capital of the valley. Its ambitious founders laid it out around broad streets in the boulevard style of great European cities and even built an imposing opera house. All that now remains of their grandiose dream is a sprawling overgrown village.

Notwithstanding Afula's overreaching, the vibrancy of Israeli culture never ceases to amaze me. Israelis read more books per capita than any other nation in the world bar one; dance, music and the theatre are thriving. Israel's orchestras and Israeli musicians are known all over the world.

Zionism's authority stems from this: in spite of the trauma of creating a new state from nothing, in spite of meagre resources and the need to invest more than 15 per cent of the national budget in defence, culture has never been forgotten. It is as if, on arrival, every Jew solemnly declared: I have lost one home but I hold its culture within me and I shall continue to develop it here as I build another home. Such fervour helps to explain why, in 1936, when there were less than 400,000 Jews in Palestine, the Israel Philharmonic Orchestra was founded under the patronage of Hubermann and Toscanini. And why, at the height of the War of Independence, when the fighting was still raging around Tel Aviv, the foundation stone of the Israel Opera was laid.

Few Israeli artists are able to support themselves primarily from their work because of the small audience available to them. They usually supplement their income with a variety of other jobs. No doubt this sometimes impairs professional standards, but it does protect and guarantee freedom of expression, the freedom to write, paint or perform whatever appeals without financial pressures. Israeli society respects its artists and writers, even though it often disagrees with what they say.

11.00 Afula

Perhaps a cup of coffee? It is only eleven o'clock and I have already seen some splendid scenery. Distances here are short. It is 44 miles from the southern end of the Golan Heights to Afula and the coast road is only another 28 miles beyond. A halt would be tempting, but today I must press on. The road is fast here, skirting barren hills whose trees were uprooted by the Turks during the First World War. The Turks needed wood to fuel their locomotives and did not spare the forests, which have never been replaced.

The coast road returns me to Israel's industrial and urban heart, looping back to within 35 miles of my home. Tel Aviv is only a short distance away and the traffic is quite heavy now, but there is no sense as yet of a great metropolis nearby. The city's northern approaches are still quite pastoral, with orchards and small farms; I have just passed a prosperous kibbutz only 10 miles from the suburbs. How long this quiet and pleasant landscape will remain before the great city consumes it under concrete and asphalt I do not know.

I was troubled at first by Frédéric Brenner's decision to photograph the shabbier and more run-down side of Tel Aviv while ignoring its glittering modern heart. On reflection, however, I realized that he was gravitating towards a particular style of architecture which dates from a time of innocence and hope. As a Frenchman he has a healthy and justified respect for old things and he knows the value of preserving them. There are skyscrapers in every city, but perhaps only in New York do they define its character. It is the buildings that Frédéric has photographed, tucked away in odd corners and quiet streets, that really matter. In Israel there is great respect for the Jewish people's ancient past but little for the architecture of our own century, which is too often demolished without a twinge of regret to make way for office blocks and shopping precincts. Europeans respect their architecture and are adept at conserving it: Israelis must learn from them if they really want to establish a cultural heritage in their new country.

For now, the sight of a cow placidly grazing in a large field just a few minutes from the heart of Tel Aviv gives me hope. There is not time, in just a day, to visit the city itself, so I cut through the suburbs to the motorway which skirts inland by way of the Ayalon Valley. After a quarter of an hour Tel Aviv is behind me. It is a fast-growing city but it isn't Cairo or London, and I hope that it does not expand to truly monstrous proportions.

13.00 Ashdod

South of Tel Aviv there are sand dunes, to which the efficient and methodical irrigation of many years has given a pleasant russet colour. This is orchard country, blue sky and bright light country, and the setting for Tel Aviv's sprawling satellite towns – Rishon Le Ziyyon, Rehovot, Ramla and others. They are too close to the metropolis to be dormitory towns; it would be more accurate to describe them as siesta towns. The sea is very close now, glinting in the sun which is already beginning to turn, though evening is still far away. A broken-down truck and some horse-drawn carts delay my arrival in Ashdod, a dynamic immigrant town and Israel's southern port, but I don't really mind because my objective is a small restaurant where they serve delicious fish. Relaxing there with a cool drink, I reflect that I am still barely 85 miles from Haifa, directly to the north, and the hardest part of the journey is still to come: the Negev, the desert.

Just south of Ashdod homesteads are still green and fertile, irrigated by water pumped all the way from the north of the country, but the ground is beginning to yellow from the loess carried on the wind from the Libyan desert. Landscapes, from a car, change almost imperceptibly. The desert creeps up, a few Bedouin encampments and kibbutzim slide by and suddenly I find myself driving alongside the Gaza Strip. Often the scene of bitter riots and demonstrations, it was occupied in the Six Day War and is home, in densely crowded refugee camps, to some half a million Palestinians crammed into barely 78 square miles. From his photographs of Gaza it is apparent that the photographer and I see it with different eyes. The soldier examining the identity card of a Palestinian in Gaza (page 157) and the look of perplexity and alarm on the face of a Palestinian toddler as an Israeli half-track rumbles by (page 158) are snapshots taken out of a larger and more complicated context surrounding the Occupied Territories.

A grim drama is unfolding here. The Palestinians do not want Israeli rule. They feel they have been robbed of their freedom and suspect they are about to be robbed of their land. However determined their resistance, Palestinians within the Occupied Territories have few leaders who can either speak for them or rein in hotheads. Their leaders are based in sovereign states abroad where they drive Mercedes limousines and patronize luxury hotels. It is these elusive figures who now speak for the thousands living in squalor in the camps. In the absence of negotiation, even the many Israelis who fervently hope that one day we will be able to extricate ourselves from the territories and give independence to their residents are forced to collude in repression which is becoming ever more heavy-handed and intransigent.

The hills have almost petered out now and I can feel the great Sinai desert, that immense sea of sand and rock, only just ahead. Not far away is Israel's most *westerly* point, Kibbutz Kerem Shalom on the Egyptian frontier. As befits its name, those who live here are indeed men of peace (*shalom*), as well as ardent socialists. I am quite alone, for there are no other cars on this stretch of road. The Negev (the word suggests dryness in Hebrew) accounts for more than 60 per cent of Israel's land mass. Experts, however, predict that with deep and accurate drilling it will be possible to uncover wells of abundant water, and judicious harnessing of the flood waters which rush through the wadis after winter rains would make it possible to irrigate a significant proportion of this wilderness.

It is a pleasant time of day to enter the desert. The light is not too glaring and it throws hills and distant objects into sharp relief, a fascinating prospect. The landscape here, on the edge of the desert, is a sea of soft sand, a bare yellow world like the Sahara – but not for long. A few miles farther on by the Egyptian border is Nizzana, formerly the crossing of the two great ancient highways of the region: the east–west road linking Egypt with Asia, and, running north–south, the spice route linking the Mediterranean with Saudi Arabia and Ethiopia. Beyond it the terrain suddenly becomes mountainous again. It is time to change gear and concentrate as the road snakes up and down through rocky passes on its way south.

The afternoon sun is behind me now, casting a riot of colours on the landscape. No better thing than to pull over, cut the engine and let the barrenness and stillness gradually permeate the spirit. It is no wonder that men of the desert feel inclined to prophesy from time to time. Here the superfluous is shed, civilization falls away and man is left alone to confront the Eternal, which he may call God, or even the Absurd, but here at least he knows what is essential and what is incidental. Sand and rock expose humanity in its nakedness, in its fundamental and necessary kernel; only the spirit remains.

The ordinary Israeli visits the desert perhaps a few dozen times in his life: first on school trips, later in the course of military service and then on family outings, usually *en route* to Eilat. But in every Israeli there is a latent awareness of the desert, just as in every Swiss there is a latent awareness of the high alpine wastes and in every Norwegian a latent awareness of the fjords and frozen wilderness of the north. The desert is a challenge to the civilization of Israel; it is also the link which binds Israel to the real Orient. It has never been properly studied. We know that in the early centuries AD it was the home of Nabataeans and Byzantines who enjoyed agricultural prosperity; the new Jewish settlements have managed to cultivate seemingly barren land with outstanding success, and no traveller in the Negev can fail to be elated by the sight – so unexpected one might think it a mirage – of bright green fields and verdant palm groves. But Israel has not yet turned to *face* the Negev; it remains at the back of the mind, precious and important but not of immediate concern. There are always items higher on the agenda than the development of the Negev.

18.00 The Negev

But back to the road and on again. I'm four hours out of Ashdod, deep in these sandy wastes, and the shadows are lengthening. No one should miss a chance to see the desert as the light fades, looking at the gathering darkness, feeling the stillness of it. On the far side of the border I can just make out Egyptian checkpoints from time to time, all proudly flying flags. Since 1981 this has been a quiet and open border where relations of cordiality and trust prevail.

And then far away, just as the light seems almost to have vanished, the hills of Eilat appear. The road dips down into a ravine, the Valley of the Moon, which really is like a lunar landscape, a chaotic and menacing vista of weirdly shaped hills unsmoothed and unsoftened by rain. This is the edge of total aridity; beyond it the desert tightens its grip and even hope is superfluous. The road broadens now, and at last, almost miraculously, I can see the glimmer of the Red Sea between black-and-white mountains like monstrous heaps of coffee and sugar. Relief at contact with the sea after long hours in the desert is always intense.

I am about to return to the Great Rift Valley which I left behind at ten o'clock this morning on the road south from the Kinneret. I have been to where two or three borders meet, and now I have arrived where four states meet – Israel, Egypt, Jordan and Saudi Arabia. This is the Gulf of Aqaba, on the Red Sea, Israel's second sea. Below me, beyond the glistening asphalt, the moonlit gulf stretches away, dotted with the lights of towns and ships; even the sky is alight as a Boeing with landing lights flashing skims over my head, perhaps on a direct flight from wintry northern Europe to this semi-tropical resort with its exotic fish and coral. This prospect, just this one alone, makes the whole of the long, desolate and tortuous journey along the Egyptian border marvellously worthwhile.

20.00 Eilat

Eilat arrives quite suddenly. One moment there is only the desert and the hum of the car, the next offices and hotels, horns and traffic and late-night shoppers. The strip is just a minute away – Eilat has many luxury hotels. It is time to sit in a bar, drink a glass of cold beer and look at the ships anchored in the bay, some on their way to Eilat, others unloading their cargo in the twin Jordanian port of Aqaba. The time is eight, eight-thirty at most. This is Israel's most *southerly* point.

This has been a one-day tour. I feel tired and in need of a shower, but I have made it in one day. I have travelled from the first light of dawn to the last light of evening. I have covered about 500 miles, from port to port, from Mediterranean to Red Sea. I have climbed to Israel's most northerly point in the snow at 7000 feet and finished my journey at its most southerly point at sea level. I have driven across valleys, through mountains and forests. I have spent long hours in the desert. The whole of my journey has been within the borders of the State of Israel that are recognized by *all* Israelis and recognized, I think, by most of the world (with the possible exception of the small region of the Golan Heights). I haven't been into the territories of the West Bank or, as others call them, Judaea and Samaria, and of course I've missed a lot. Jerusalem, in particular, but I shall make a special visit there later in the book.

I want my tour to convey the extreme contrast in landscape and climate. Take average rainfall as an example: Eilat gets little more than an inch of rain a year; the corresponding figure in the north of the country is 60 inches. In spite of its variety, however, Israel is a single geographical and historical entity, and anyone who examines it carefully and loves it dearly will recognize the signs that make it one. They will find signs of the desert in the sand dunes outside Tel Aviv and the curves of the rolling hills of Judaea in the Negev. Such extremes provide a certain element of drama in living here, a sense of abrupt transitions. The question to ask is not what the Jews have done, are doing and will do to the landscape of their ancestral homeland, but what the landscape of the ancestral homeland has done and is doing to them after forty years of statehood.

CHAPTER FOUR

THE MAZE OF IDENTITY

Suddenly a man rises in the morning
And feels that he is a people, and begins to walk.

AMIR GILBOA

Three ghostly characters are currently to be found hovering in the atmosphere of Israel. They intermingle and sometimes create no small degree of confusion. They are the Jew, the Israeli and the Zionist. If you stop passers-by in the street and ask them to describe themselves in these terms you will get a variety of strange replies comprehensible only with a thorough knowledge of the assumptions behind both the speaker and the characters themselves.

One passer-by will say that he is a Jew and that Israeliness is just the shell of citizenship that encloses him. Another will declare the opposite: his Israeliness is the most important and deeply felt element in his personality, while his Jewishness is altogether vague. A third will claim for himself the adjective "Zionist" and even give it pride of place in the scheme of his identity, while a fourth will firmly declare that Zionism is quite irrelevant. A fifth may define Jewishness in purely religious terms, which will lead him finally to admit that he cannot be considered a Jew; a sixth will insist that his Jewishness and Israeliness are of equal importance and will also claim a strong sense of Zionism, and so on and so on. Are these three concepts so nebulous as to be beyond definition, so that we can re-create them in our own image from day to day? Or is their versatility the key to their power, allowing each of us to find a stable identity within them?

Now released to some extent from the demands of mere survival, Israelis have more time to ask themselves who, exactly, they think they are. The astonishing and unprecedented flowering of literature, theatre and cinema in recent years is an unmistakable sign. Novels, collections of short stories and volumes of poetry sell thousands of copies, out of all proportion to the relatively small number of readers in Israel. There is a healthy market for literary and socio-political magazines. Theatres are always full and cultural activity in general is vibrant. Informed observers believe this to be evidence not of a consumer society hungry for aesthetics but of a society hungry to explore its *identity*. Secular Israeli society, for example, is much more preoccupied with culture and art than religious society, for whom questions of identity are less pressing.

I do not believe that a description of Israel after forty years is possible without an attempt to explain who these three elemental national characters are.

What is a Jew?

Every few years this question surfaces to galvanize national politics. Governments have foundered in its wake and Jews from all over the world have an opinion on the subject. Few people have forgotten the comprehensive referendum which David Ben-Gurion once called to canvass opinion among the most learned Jews in Israel and the Diaspora. Relations with the Reform and Conservative Jewish congregations risk crisis over the issue. In fact, the definition of a Jew in Israeli law has changed three times in the last forty years. To a non-Jewish observer the whole thing might seem ridiculous: three thousand years later, and they still can't decide who they are! But the very fact that three thousand years have failed to produce a unanimous answer to so fundamental a question proves just how difficult the concept of Jewishness is and how thick a shell of religious tradition it acquired during the centuries of the Diaspora. The waning of religion which has swept across the Western world in the past two hundred years has also cracked the Jewish shell and exposed the national component within. The old certainties are no longer enough.

Many people strongly object to the state's involvement in such matters. In their opinion Israel needs only to define an Israeli, and the Rabbinical Law will decide who is a Jew. But Israel has been compelled to define Jewishness because a fundamental law, the Law of Return, which confers rights of Israeli citizenship on every Jew in the Diaspora, requires a clear prior definition of Jewish identity.

For the first twelve years of the state's existence, the years of mass immigration, the definition of a Jew in the Law of Return was as follows: a Jew is one who declares himself to be so when applying for citizenship of the state. A wide and easily accessible door was thus opened to the world. The genius of David Ben-Gurion was his recognition that to use the ancient Rabbinical formula – a Jew is the son of a Jewish mother or one who has converted in accordance with the law – would do serious injustice to many genuine Jews who, while not exactly fitting these criteria, had suffered cruelly in the Holocaust and displayed an unequivocal Jewish identity in their lives.

Subsequently, under pressure from religious opinion, the definition was changed to accord with Rabbinical Law, and today the Law of Return defines a Jew as one who is the son of a Jewish mother or has converted (without defining the form such conversion may take). This begs the deeply controversial question: is conversion in accordance with Rabbinical Law the only conversion recognized by the State of Israel, or will it accept conversions performed by Reform or Conservative rabbis, especially in the United States?

Such controversies fail to conceal the real problem inherent in defining Jewishness: the astonishing *emptiness* of the definition. Whether a Jew is one who declares himself to be a Jew, according to the broad secular-nationalist definition, or is one whose mother is a Jew, in the religious version, *both* definitions are equally vacuous. A Jew doesn't need to live in Israel to retain his Jewish identity, he doesn't need to speak Hebrew or any other language to be considered a Jew, he doesn't need to belong to a Jewish community (even at the formal level of holding an identity card or passport) to be called a Jew. A Jew doesn't need to perform any religious duties or even to believe in God to be a Jew. To define a Jew even in accordance with religious law is a definition of national attribution (at its most basic level) and is quite different from any definition of a Christian or a Muslim, which invokes a religious attribution without reference to nationality.

A Jew who lives in the Bahamas, for example, the son of a Christian father and a Jewish mother, married to a Christian and accompanying her and his Christian children to church every Sunday, who doesn't speak a word of Hebrew and, if asked where Israel is, hasn't a clue which page to turn to in the atlas, a man who doesn't know any other Jew and who has no links with any Jewish congregation – *he*, according to Rabbinical Law, is just as Jewish as the Chief Rabbi of Israel. Such a person is no freak or aberration: at one level or another perhaps two or three million Jews in Western Europe and the Soviet Union are not very different. Trotsky, an atheistic revolutionary, was as Jewish as the arch-capitalist Baron de Rothschild even though they had nothing in common: not language, not culture, not nationality and least of all political ideology. The Chief Rabbi of the United Hebrew Congregations of the British Commonwealth is no more Jewish than Daniel Cohn-Bendit, the anarchist of German extraction who led the *événements* in Paris in 1968.

Jewishness (not Judaism, which is a function of culture and tradition) is thus an act of identification with the Jewish people without any obligation to active participation. On the other hand, and this must be constantly stressed, being a Jew is *not* open to racial definition, since someone not born to a Jewish mother can still become a Jew and a Jew can stop being a Jew. In spite of fatuous statements about "Jewish destiny", it was possible in the past and is still possible today to leave the Jewish congregation without any difficulty: over the centuries countless thousands of Jews have assimilated into whatever nation they lived in. Compare that with the millions in the world today who are compelled to be nationals of the state that has rights to their ancestral lands – in Russia, India, China and elsewhere. In other words, together with the vacuity inherent in any definition of a Jew there is also a strong element of *freedom*. A Jew is a Jew because he chooses to be a Jew and not because he is obliged to be a Jew. Even a Jew born to a Jewish mother can become a Christian or a Muslim and renounce his Jewish identity.

This ambivalence is and always has been inherent in Jewishness and is the root cause of much pathological anti-Semitism. It leads the Jew to vacillate between the self-hatred and sense of moral superiority so characteristic of the mentality of many Jews. It is a burden that the State of Israel as the state of the Jews must carry, though the very existence of the state offers a historic solution in *Israeliness*. However, between the Jew and the Israeli stands the Zionist.

What is a Zionist?

Until 1948 a Zionist was someone who wanted to establish a Jewish state in Greater Israel. Since the creation of the State of Israel, a Zionist is someone who believes that the state belongs not only to its citizens but *also* to the Jewish people. The Law of Return could not express this more clearly.

The State of Israel, of course, belongs primarily to its citizens, holders of Israeli identity cards, Jews and Palestinians, Druse and Circassians, all those who have the right to vote and determine by parliamentary means the laws and governance of the state. But although they are the first and most important owners of the state, they are not, according to a Zionist, its sole owners. The state was created to give self-determination to the 700,000 Jews who were already in Palestine in 1948 and also to address the problem of the Diaspora. Henceforth, every Jew in the world would have a homeland offering him rights of residence and citizenship should he choose to exercise them. The Law of Return unequivocally requires the State of Israel to accept every Jew whether it needs him or not, whether it has employment for him or not. There is nothing comparable in the immigration policy of any other country in the world.

This is the essence of Zionism. It is not an ideological conspectus. It is not bound to one form of government or another. Someone can be a socialist Zionist, capitalist Zionist, fascist Zionist or religious Zionist. If the State of Israel had remained within the borders of the 1947 partition, it would be no less Zionist than the State of Israel within its present borders. If the Occupied Territories are returned to the Palestinians, the State of Israel will be Zionist to the same degree. An Israeli citizen can be loyal and patriotic without being a Zionist, just as Druse citizens sacrifice and continue to sacrifice their lives for the security of the state, as do those few Israeli Jews who reject Zionism. Among Jews of the Diaspora, only those who see the State of Israel also as their state can really be counted Zionists.

The Zionism of the state is not only a matter of the Law of Return. From time to time, national interests must give way to the interests of Jews in the Diaspora. Thus, for example, Israel is hesitating to open relations with the Soviet Union so long as its present emigration policies continue, and Israel insisted on freedom for Syrian Jews as a condition of military disengagement after the Yom Kippur War in 1974, a demand which, however, did not succeed.

When they attack Zionism (if this is what they are actually attacking), few Arabs realize that when a Palestinian state is established it will need to adopt similar principles. Any new state will be one for *all* Palestinians, even for those born elsewhere and living in exile. For them and them alone, once the state has settled the question: what is a Palestinian? No Jew could ever find this a racist principle.

What is an Israeli?

"Israeli" is both an expression of citizenship and of identity, just as one might use the terms "Briton", "Spaniard" or "Hungarian". Taking citizenship at its most basic level, a person who holds an Israeli identity card is an Israeli, just as an American citizen is one who holds an American passport which gives him rights of residency even if he speaks no English and has never set foot in the United States. A great variety of people hold Israeli identity cards: they include not only Jews loyal to the state but even convicted Palestinian terrorists who, after serving their sentences, enjoy rights of citizenship as valid as those of any other Israeli citizen.

But, of course, to be an Israeli is not only a question of citizenship but of identity. In this context it expresses the Jewish *totality*. If you happened to meet Moses the Lawgiver and asked him to describe himself he would probably say: I am an Israeli(te), or, I am a son of the people of Israel. If you persisted and asked Moses:

are you a Jew? he would reply: I don't understand what you mean, the term "Jew" is not familiar to me.

You could have the same conversation with the Judges Gideon, Deborah and Jephtah, with King David and his son Solomon, with the Prophets Elijah, Isaiah and Micah and Amos, in short with all the leading figures of the Old Testament. It was the name "Israeli(te)" which first identified the Jewish people and according to tradition the name was given to us by God Himself – in the book of Genesis, chapter 32: "And he said unto him, What is thy name? And he said, Jacob. And he said, Thy name shall be called no more Jacob, but Israel: for as a prince hast thou power with god and with men, and hast prevailed." The word "Jew" is used to identify an Israeli(te) for the first time in the Book of Esther, which describes the Jewish exile of the fifth or fourth century BC: "Now in Shushan the palace there was a certain Jew, whose name was Mordecai." Only when the Israeli(te) found himself cast out from the Land of Israel, separated from his language and the affirmative culture of his people and living amid another people, did he begin to be called a Jew. And as the Diaspora spread through the centuries, so he began to see himself through Gentile eyes and acted accordingly (to paraphrase Jean-Paul Sartre). Judeaus, Jude, Juif, Jew: and yet Israeli(te) is now restored to the homeland.

When the Jewish state was established, its name was chosen quite naturally and without dissent. The early settlers could have called it Judaea, or Zion or even the State of the Jews as envisaged by Herzl. "Israel", it was thought almost unanimously, expressed the return to the ancient Jewish totality which had been realized in full once before in history and had existed only in hope through the long centuries of the Diaspora. There are, however, many Jews in Israel who feel that "Israeli" implies citizenship and not identity. They prefer "Jewish-Israeli", and for two reasons: first, to distinguish themselves from those, like Palestinians, whose citizenship is Israeli but whose essential identity is not; and, secondly, so as not to distance themselves from non-Israeli Jews living in the Diaspora. But the combination is often confusing, since there is no knowing whether "Jewish" is added to "Israeli" as an expression of religious or national identity, and if the latter in what sense? Jewish visitors often complain that Israel doesn't feel Jewish, as if Israel could be anything other than a Jewish state in everything it does.

Forty years of statehood have failed to assign clear roles to our three ghostly characters, the Jew, the Israeli and the Zionist. If anything, they have made it even harder for them to describe themselves. If you asked an Englishman to define Englishness, he might say that Englishness is expressed in everything around him: in the English light and fog, the constant drizzle, the English language and literature, the English pub and of course (alas!) English food. Then there are parliamentary traditions, a half-ironic and half-reverential attitude to the monarchy, the peculiar helmets policemen wear and their reluctance to carry firearms, the passions aroused by football and cricket, and the affected Woosterish accents which are still sometimes thought a mark of good breeding, though not often of intelligence. In short, any identity is made up of many thousands of indefinable threads, and even someone who has never heard of Shakespeare is no less English if these gossamer threads enwrap his personality.

So it is in Israel. The vacuity behind the question: what is a Jew? is now filled with qualities, identities, hints and meanings so various and of such vital tangibility that Jews are often alarmed. Unlike Jews in the Diaspora, Israelis can no longer content themselves with theories and abstractions: they must produce an applicable and practical solution to immediate problems. They must decide, for example, the precise angle at which Israeli soldiers should hold their weapons when confronting violent but unarmed Palestinian demonstrators in Gaza, Nablus or Hebron. The angle determines the trajectory of the projectile that is fired: is it one designed only to intimidate, or to kill? Their decision will say more about the quality of Jewish justice than any number of lofty quotations from the Talmud. So it is with thousands of other things: should we buy another tank in the interests of security or endow a cultural centre in a remote settlement? How wide should the corridors be in government offices and what is the correct size of prison cells? Should we sell weapons to South Africa and so provide work for munitions factories in Galilee or should we support sanctions as a gesture against apartheid and accept the consequences of higher unemployment?

Questions of this kind do not always concern Jews in the Diaspora, whose lives are mapped by the non-Jewish society in which they live. Their part in national life is a French or an American or a Mexican part, not a Jewish one. Discovering one's Jewish identity in exile is a matter of plotting the *border* that separates Jew from non-Jew: how is the Jew to preserve what is important to him in an alien culture which surrounds him like a sea? The questions that preoccupy the total Jew, the Israeli, are questions of *meaning*. Jewish identity in Western society has become conveniently malleable and the vacuity inherent in much of it does not bear close examination. What may be salving to the Diaspora is not so to Israel, where our three ghostly characters continue to sow discord at every opportunity. Forty years of statehood have not yet enabled them to explain themselves, but they have produced a genuine reality, for better or worse.

CHAPTER FIVE

JERUSALEM–THE WALL AND THE HILL

Outside – Jerusalem: city of Abraham's glorious trial,
Where he bound his son on one of the hills:
That fire, kindled at dawn, still burns on the hill,
The rains have not put it out: it is the fire between
The sacrificial pieces.

URI ZVI GREENBERG

When I was about fifteen or sixteen, I remember reading Dostoevsky's *Crime and Punishment* one winter Sabbath in Jerusalem. I was engrossed in the scene near the end where Raskolnikov walks across St Petersburg on his way to the police station where he intends finally to confess to his crime. And then I came to these lines:

> In the middle of the square he knelt down, bowed to the earth, and kissed the muddy ground with joy and rapture, rose and bowed again:
>
> "He's had a skinful" – remarked a lad nearby.
>
> There was laughter.
>
> "He's going to Jerusalem, boys, that's where he's going. Saying goodbye to his children and his homeland, bowing down to the whole world, kissing St Petersburg, the royal capital, and its earth" – added a tipsy citizen.

I stopped reading, astonished and confused and even a little agitated. What is Jerusalem doing here? I looked up from the page and through the window to the silent little Sabbath streets bathed in the sunlight of Jerusalem, but I could not connect them with the gloomy streets of St Petersburg a century before and the tormented student-murderer making his way along them. Was it really *this* Jerusalem, of which I felt so natural a part, that was referred to? I was suddenly flushed with pride, as if in a mysterious way I too had entered into the book and become a character in it.

Many great literary or musical works arouse similar feelings in me – Bach's Passions, the Requiems of Berlioz and Verdi, Monteverdi's glorious "Vespero della Beata Virgina". Jerusalem has been celebrated in music and poetry throughout history and I first understood, all those years ago that winter Sabbath, that this grey city, this somewhat provincial city with its mean streets and little houses, is not just a city but a symbol transcending the frontiers of the Jewish world. Jerusalem is deeply ingrained in the culture of the West.

For Jews, especially, Jerusalem is an immensely more powerful symbol than is Israel. It encapsulates all spirituality, the memory of the past and the great hope. During the long years of exile the toast was never "Next year in Israel" but "Next year in Jerusalem", as if Jerusalem contained Israel and not vice versa. Elderly Jews who came to Israel to die chose Jerusalem so that they could be buried on the Mount of Olives, the very place where the Messiah will return to redeem the world. No wonder, then, that by the mid nineteenth century Jews formed the majority of the city's population.

Jerusalem's hold on the imagination has always overshadowed Israel's. It is appropriately symbolic that Zionism – before Herzl had even begun to think about the "State of the Jews" – was born in the late 1870s when a group of pious Jews left

Jerusalem for the swamps of Malabes on the coastal plain where they built the first settlement since the destruction of the Second Temple, the mother of settlements – Petah Tiqwa (Gate of Hope). In order to establish the reality of Greater Israel and take the first steps towards the eventual creation of the State of Israel, those pious men and women had first to distance themselves from the symbol of abstract Jewish spirituality in the image of Jerusalem.

That was many years ago now, and both the State of Israel and Jerusalem have changed enormously. Yet they remain inextricably linked and the relationship between them is as good a way as any of taking the blood pressure of Zionism. Jerusalem, the Jewish spiritual heart, should have no adverse effect on the free flow of new ideas, the normalization vital to the proper functioning of Zionism. Excessive emotional investment in Jerusalem is not a healthy sign.

I do not mean, however, to detract from Jerusalem either as symbol or reality. Perhaps a few words about my own background will show why. I am a fifth-generation native of Jerusalem. My grandfather's grandfather, a poor rabbi, arrived in Jerusalem in the middle of the nineteenth century from Salonika, then in Turkish hands, where a flourishing Jewish community made up the majority of the city (the only city outside Palestine of which this was true). He left his home and his community not because of any anti-Semitic pressure but solely out of love for Jerusalem. My maternal grandfather, a wealthy merchant of Mogador in Morocco, made the same journey in the early 1930s, leaving all his property and his grown-up children behind. My father wrote twelve books describing in detail the way of life and customs of the Sephardi communities in Jerusalem at the beginning of this century. These books were written as a labour of love and they reflect meticulous scholarship. I, too, have a special relationship with Jerusalem and often write about it in stories and novels. Yet in recent years I have begun to feel that the Jewish people's deep identification with Jerusalem, and its role as a symbol of unity, wholeness and liberation, can no longer go unquestioned.

Jerusalem has, without doubt, a special place in the Jewish heart. Its qualities and atmosphere are immensely evocative, the more so since reunification in 1967. Money for development has poured in, parts of the town have been transformed and, in large measure because of the inspiration of Teddy Kollek, its mayor, the city is now a treasure for people everywhere of whatever nationality, custom or creed.

Jerusalem was the capital of Palestine under the British Mandate and on partition in November 1947 it saw some of the fiercest fighting in the War of Independence. Combat was hand to hand and house to house, the Arabs losing territory in West Jerusalem and the Jews being forced to abandon their ancient quarter in the Old City where they had lived for centuries. The whole Jewish sector was under siege for weeks; there were heavy losses in the fighting to relieve it. With the signing of the cease-fire agreement in mid 1949 the city was cut in half: concrete walls and barbed-wire fences went up and watchtowers were built along the minefields which divided the Jordanian–Palestinian sector in the east from the Jewish sector.

There was only one crossing point, reserved exclusively for foreign pilgrims. For nineteen years Jerusalem remained two separate worlds, closed against each other. Israel declared the city its capital and the seat of government, with the Knesset and Presidential residence. On the other side of the wire was a provincial Jordanian town.

The Six Day War did not start in Jerusalem: the focus of the conflict and the events that sparked it off were far away in the southern Sinai peninsula. With the unexpected Jordanian intervention in the war, however, and the bombardment of the Jewish sector, fighting promptly erupted in the heart of the city. Here, at least, the battle was brief and decisive: in the course of a lightning two-day campaign the eastern sector was overrun and the city reunited.

I say *reunited* and not *liberated* because the Arabs of East Jerusalem did not welcome the Israelis as, say, Parisians welcomed the Allies in 1944. The city was *only* reunited: the barbed wire and concrete came down, telephones were reconnected, broken water mains repaired. The city simply reverted to what it had been nineteen years before, as it had been during all the years of its existence – one city.

That Jerusalem is one city is an undisputed fact. Another fact is that it is the capital of Israel. It was so even when it was divided and there was no reason that it should not remain so after reunification. This, too, is a fact but it is not the final fact; there are two more.

Jerusalem is, first, a city of deep religious significance. For Christians, it is the site of the crucifixion and resurrection, as Christians believe, of Jesus of Nazareth. For Muslims, it is where the Qubbet es-Sakhra was built in the seventh century over the rock from which Muslims believe the Prophet ascended to Heaven (hence its popular name, the Dome of the Rock). To Muslims the city ranks third in holiness after Mecca and Medina.

Secondly, it is a city of central importance to Palestinian Arabs of whom more than a hundred thousand live in Jerusalem today.

What do these facts tell us about the future?

In the original United Nations partition plan of 1947, Jerusalem was given international status with a neutral administration to arbitrate the various and conflicting claims of its citizens. Both Jews and Arabs instinctively rejected the proposal, however, believing it inconceivable that a living city should be turned over to the dead hand of Swedish, Australian or Guinean bureaucrats. The city belonged and still belongs to its residents and only they can manage it. On the other hand, the whole world has a claim to Jerusalem and Israel cannot behave as if the city were its exclusive property. The holy places of Christianity and Islam must be tended by their adherents in an atmosphere of harmony and freedom of worship. Arabs have rights in a city (which they call El-Quds, "Holy") of national significance to them.

In spite of its reunification, therefore, Jerusalem's future *must* lie in administration by two civilian authorities, Jewish and Arab, both equally respected. Berlin remains under the direction of the two superpower blocs because any friction there is likely to have fatal and irrevocable consequences. In the same way, Jerusalem will remain the living seismograph of war and peace in the Middle East. The future of Greater Israel is the future of Jerusalem: a free and open city with no borders but shared between two administrations and respecting the rights of all its different communities. The European Community is on the verge of allowing the free movement of citizens among its member states. Something similar needs to be adopted in Jerusalem, and tomorrow will not be a moment too soon.

Later in the book (pages 110–11) there is Frédéric Brenner's fine photograph of the Western Wall, the last relic of the Temple which was destroyed when the city was sacked by Titus in AD 70. It was inaccessible to Jews for nineteen years; they returned to it after the Six Day War and here they stand and pray over the ruins of the past and hopes for the future. The Wall stands at the foot of the magnificent mosque of El Aqsa and the Dome of the Rock; the Church of the Holy Sepulchre is just a few streets away. Muslims in Jerusalem have fine mosques and Christians have churches full of glittering liturgical images; Jews have only a bare stone wall whose significance is *restraint*. They are forbidden to rebuild the Temple until the Messiah himself comes to redeem the world. There is something significant in the sight of Jews, now the largest community and dominant power in the city, standing before a monument radiating restraint and asceticism. A wall, a high stone barrier, nothing more. Restraint and asceticism are salutary qualities in a ruler; and the bareness, architectural modesty and abstract nature of the Western Wall may perhaps encourage such qualities in a people now returned to its homeland and ruling others there.

Outside the city to the west stands the hill – Mount Herzl. This is now the arena for the national ceremonies of the State of Israel, in the new city which sprang up in the mid nineteenth century under the impetus of Zionism. Complementary symbols confirm the reality of Israel's existence today: the Yad Vashem Memorial to the victims of the Holocaust, the floor of its Memorial Hall inlaid with the names of the extermination camps; the military cemetery and the Tomb of the Unknown Soldier; and not least the tomb of Herzl himself and the graves of the fellow founders of Zionism.

The old walled city at the heart of Jerusalem has long been divided into four quarters: Jewish, Arab, Christian and Armenian. Here, among the sacred sites and holy relics, Israel is no more than a steward or trustee. The ancient fathers of the Jewish people, the great and inspired men who made this city the heart and focus of the Old Testament, were not kings or generals; they were angry prophets, perpetual dissidents and scourges of authority. It is their human greatness which made this city the inheritance of humanity and not just of the Jews.

Amid the fear and uncertainty before the Six Day War, the most popular song of the time – "Jerusalem of Gold" – was first heard at a choral festival a few weeks before hostilities began. People everywhere fell in love with it, humming along without the faintest suspicion that its words would soon come true and the hidden half of Jerusalem would be restored to them. The last photograph in this book is a classic view of Jerusalem from the cemetery on the Mount of Olives, at sunrise when the city is radiating gold – the gold of the rising sun, the gold of the Dome of the Rock, the gold of the medieval walls. There is no reason to divide Jerusalem again.

CHAPTER SIX

ONE HOMELAND, TWO PEOPLES, TWO STATES?

The old one hurries along. The drivers are switching on their engines. This is all he needs, to be left overnight in this arboreal silence. Before he goes he would just like to hear the warden's opinion of the dumb Arab. The truck driver has got it into his head that the man is laying in a stock of kerosene . . .

The fire warden is stirred. "Kerosene?"

"Probably that bloody driver's fantasy. This Arab's a placid sort, isn't he?"

"Wonderfully placid," the warden quickly agrees. Then he walks around the old man and whispers confidentially: "Isn't he a local?"

"Local?"

"Because our forest is growing over, well, over a ruined village . . ."

Facing the Forests, A. B. YEHOSHUA

I wrote *Facing the Forests* in 1962, some years before the Six Day War and the emergence of the Palestinian problem. The story tells of a perpetual student, a bachelor who has been postponing completion of his thesis for many years and who, on the advice of friends believing he needs solitude, takes a job as a fire warden in a forest planted by the Israeli National Fund. In his watchtower he finds an old Arab, a mute, already in residence with his little granddaughter. The student arrives with his books and notebooks and tries to concentrate in the silence but to no avail, because his inability to concentrate is internal. His frustration mounts and he spends much time roaming the forest, beginning to forge a wordless relationship with the Arab who turns out to be a local man, the forest having been planted over the ruins of his village which was destroyed in the War of Independence. The Arab intends to burn the forest down. It is dedicated to all kinds of Jewish benefactors who have donated funds in order to perpetuate their names on memorial plaques among the trees.

The old Arab, who is secretly stockpiling kerosene, is afraid at first of the young intellectual who follows him everywhere. But the warden, eaten up by his loneliness and failure to write a single line of his thesis, finds a kind of mad release in encouraging the Arab in his plans. Quietly, though never openly, he supports him. When the Arab does eventually set fire to the forest the warden is unable to raise the alarm in time because, before scattering his kerosene, the Arab cuts the telephone lines to the watchtower. He is promptly arrested, his futile destructive gesture not, as he imagines, somehow re-creating his lost village. The "student", whom the police suspect to be the real culprit, is sent home in disgrace.

I intended *Facing the Forests* not only as a political fable but also as an exploration of a difficult state of mind. I was interested in the dangers of repression, and in the links between self-repression and that exercised by whole nations and peoples. Repression ultimately finds release in destruction, in the story through a temporary alliance between a frustrated individual on the fringes of society and an avenging enemy outside it.

That was more than twenty-five years ago, and the Arab-Israeli dispute, many aspects of which we had all repressed, has since surfaced with a vengeance. One of the surest signs is linguistic. Palestinians no longer call Israelis "Jews who live in Palestine" but now simply refer to them as Israelis. Israelis have stopped calling Palestinians "Arabs of Greater Israel" but refer to them as Palestinians. To agree on the naming of names is hardly a solution, but it is a first and necessary step towards one. The Palestinian problem is recognized in the Middle East and the world at large as the core of the Arab-Israeli dispute, a problem which overshadows all others facing the State of Israel. I do not consider it the most complex of the problems central to our lives, but it is the most urgent problem.

Let me be clear: the land called Israel by Jews and Palestine by Arabs is shared between two peoples who, although technically related as they are both of Semitic origin, are quite distinct in language, history and tradition. Each one is entitled to self-determination.

"My people were here some fifteen hundred years before you arrived," a Jew might say to an Arab. "Our spiritual tradition was born here and the traces of our history are everywhere. The whole world knows it."

"But, my friend," the Arab replies, "as long ago as the time of the Second Temple you began to leave this place. When my people came here in the mid seventh century we found a tiny number of Jews living under Byzantine rule, and no one ever suggested we were trespassing on Jewish land. You did not return for centuries. By 1917, the year of the Balfour Declaration, there were more than half a million of us and only 50,000 of you, and some of those would never have come had not a Turkish despot prevented us from resisting your arrival."

"I cannot agree. Palestine has never existed as an independent entity. You saw yourselves as just a part of an Arab world where your brothers in other countries spoke the same language and shared the same culture and traditions. A large number of you came here in this century at the same time as us, to a land for the most part desolate and neglected. Jordan is also part of the original Palestine. A million of your compatriots live there in peace and harmony. There is plenty of room for all of you over the border."

"True, I am part of the Arab world but only an ignoramus could think it homogeneous. Each people has its own identity and homeland. My identity is tied to Palestine, and how I see myself in relation to the Arab world is my business. You don't deny that it is a Swede's business how he sees himself in relation to Scandinavia, or a Czech's where he stands in relation to Slavs, do you? Palestine is my homeland. My fathers' forefathers lived here and the desert and the swamps and the wilderness are part of my identity. Whenever you start digging in search of your precious ancient history the first things you find are the tombs of my ancestors and the foundations of our mosques."

"No one wants to dispossess you or drive you out of your homeland," the Jew counters. "Anyone who thinks that Zionism didn't consider the Arab issue at the turn of the century has got it all wrong. Before the Holocaust, we thought that five to seven million Jews would come here and we wanted you, half a million of you, to live in peace and harmony with all your rights protected. Read Herzl or the fathers of Zionism and you will see how much they respected you and wanted you to be partners. You know what happened in the 1920s and '30s: your hostility persuaded the British to curtail immigration and millions of my people perished. After the Holocaust, with a third of our number exterminated, we Jews understood what it is like to be a people without a homeland."

"What happened in Europe was unspeakable, I know that, but we Arabs aren't responsible for it. We didn't cause the Holocaust and we don't have to atone for it now. Find yourself somewhere else!"

"But there *isn't* anywhere else! This is the land of our prayers and dreams throughout all the years of our exile. Of course you're not to blame for the Holocaust but you know perfectly well that the Jewish problem didn't begin with the Holocaust, nor end with it. The Jewish problem is for the whole world. Remember, we Jews have lived in Arab countries too, where we were oppressed and persecuted minorities. How can you fail to see that we should have a homeland like any other people? There is nowhere else but here. I repeat, no one wants to dispossess a single Arab. You are enjoying and will continue to enjoy the fruits of the prosperity that we Jews are striving for."

The Arab is not convinced. "I don't deny that you have done a great deal for all of us here, but I know how it will end. Arabs will become second-class citizens. As Jewish immigration continues, we'll end up as a helpless minority dependent on your charity. No, I don't want more Jews here and I can do without your charity."

"Then let us divide the land between us. Where I live will be my state and where you live will be yours."

By the end of the 1930s, Zionists realized that the ground was falling away from under the feet of European Jewry and that the establishment of a Jewish state was therefore an immediate necessity. Since then, many formulas for partition of one kind or another have been put to the Palestinians. They have rejected every one. They were and for the most part still are convinced that they are under no obligation to share their homeland with anyone. To them, Zionism was just the creed of a vocal minority, no more. Eventually, in desperation after the Holocaust, the Jews of Palestine agreed to the partition plan adopted by the United Nations. This gave them only some 6200 out of western Palestine's 10,400 square miles, the greater part of the territory allotted to them being barren desert.

The plan was turned down flat by the Palestinians and their Arab brothers who swore to erase with their blood what they considered totally unjust. In the war of 1947–9 the Palestinians were defeated, despite the support of their allies, and part of the land originally allotted to them under the terms of the partition – about 1500 square miles – was annexed by Israel. The greater part of the remainder (the West Bank) was ceded to Jordan and a small area (the Gaza Strip) to Egypt. Thousands of refugees fled their homes and were dispersed in camps, adding a new and severe problem which has since come to symbolize the bitter injustice Palestinians have always felt done to them. There were not many refugees at first, but their presence at all was a standing reproach to any notion of conciliation. States all over the Arab world took up their cause and soon decided to avenge an eye with an eye.

Until the refugee problem was solved, there was no question of any Arab compromising with a Jewish state whose legitimacy, in any case, he did not recognize. Arab strategy ran as follows: we have lost one battle in a long war. We can afford to lose many more battles, we have unlimited resources. But the moment you Jews lose one single battle, your fate will be sealed.

In 1967 the Six Day War erupted and the Israelis, well aware of the truth of this logic, won yet another battle and occupied the remainder of western Greater Israel, a farther 2700 square miles. But this time the Palestinians had learned the lesson of the 1948 war and there was no repeat of the flight into refugee camps. The decisive majority clung resolutely to their land. Three-quarters of a million Palestinians now live within the Green Line or pre-1967 borders (in theory with rights of citizenship equal to those of Israelis) and a further million and a quarter live in the territories occupied during the war, some in refugee camps. What is to be done?

At first Israel offered a compromise, a partial restoration of territory. It was refused. Having just suffered a humiliating defeat, Arabs everywhere were determined on another, more successful war to erase the memory of the last. They were certain, too, that militant states like Syria and Egypt would force the entire Arab world into a collective, life-or-death confrontation with Israel. But it has not happened that way. The passing years, the aftermath of the Yom Kippur War, peace with Egypt, *de facto* peace with Jordan and interim agreements with Syria, Israel's acceptance in the eyes of the West and in some quarters of the Third World – nothing has given Palestinians any cause for hope. They feel trapped, and the voices now emerging from the camps are prepared to reconsider the old offers of compromise, rejected long ago, offers to return to the United Nations partition plan of 1947 or even to the Green Line.

The two sides remain locked in confrontation, exchanging rapiers, one of which is poisoned, like Hamlet and Laertes. In 1948 the state had 650,000 Jews and 160,000 non-Jews; today the figures are 3,561,000 and 2,175,000 (of which 775,000 are within the Green Line) respectively. One in three people in Greater Israel is Palestinian, but the Palestinian population is younger and growing more quickly. In another twenty years the ratio will be one in two. Israelis believe they can circumvent the "demographic menace" by encouraging a vast increase in immigration, failing which they will have to "persuade" a proportion of the Palestinians to leave for Jordan and elsewhere. Palestinians, on the other hand, believe that terrorism, the threat of total war, stubborn adherence to their property rights through the courts and a swiftly increasing population will inexorably give them the upper hand. Meanwhile the world looks on wearily, just as it has watched the Irish conflict for so long.

Shared realities are, however, emerging. Economic programmes bring Jew and Palestinian together, and in spite of all the troubles the West Bank is developing rapidly. Money from Arab states, perhaps compensation for their reluctance to intervene militarily, is opening new hospitals and building new universities. Palestinians are beginning to learn Hebrew and participate to an encouraging extent in the fabric of Jewish life. Jews in their turn are wrestling with Arabic and becoming more and more Oriental. Cultural barriers are falling here and there, and Palestinians have learned how to use Israeli democracy to fight for their rights. But as in any state shared between two peoples, no contact, however close, can offset the desire of each to preserve its identity nor the fear that one will swallow and destroy the other. Over the years, myths and stereotypes have given way to a certain amount of mutual understanding. But deep distrust remains.

What is to be done?

The gap between Paradise and Hell is sometimes so narrow as to inspire both pessimism and optimism. This is how I feel as an Israeli about the whole bitter conflict, and it is why I and countless others campaign with mingled fatigue and hope for the only possible solution: *partition into two states.*

It is still possible: Israel is not yet Northern Ireland where Catholics and Protestants are inextricably interwoven. There are still extensive areas in western Greater Israel which are emphatically Jewish and others which are no less Palestinian. It *is* possible to divide, to establish a border and let each people consolidate its identity, though the decision will not be easy nor its implementation painless. Not a few Jewish Israelis would prefer to drive the Palestinians out. There are strategic complications and new Jewish settlements in the territories whose occupants may be reluctant to leave. Deep-rooted historical memories, the heavy sacrifices of successive wars and a profound distrust of the other side lead many Israelis to question the wisdom of any compromise at all. They *must* compromise.

The border need be no more formidable than the border which divides Belgium and Holland. No need for barbed wire, minefields and armed checkpoints, just an invisible but very real line. A human imagination capable of inventing the computer and putting space stations into orbit can surely devise administrative arrangements allowing the Palestinian and the Israeli to feel that all of Israel and all of Palestine are open to him, while his own state, in which he can live exactly as he wishes, is defined and enclosed within a part of this total territory.

One country, two peoples and therefore two states. I can see no other solution. The Palestinian state can indeed be linked in one way or another with Jordan, in which about a million Palestinians live, but that will be decided after partition. The Arab world, in the past so resolutely opposed to compromise, is coming to realize that there is *no alternative* – the same call behind Zionism in its early days.

That is what I hope and believe the future will bring, but what will it bring to the spirit of the State of Israel? On looking at the history of Zionism and the last forty years, and at the absolute ground zero from which it all started, I am bound to admit that the State of Israel is so far a story of outstanding success.

A tragic success, certainly. Tragic because if the State of Israel had been established twenty years before 1948, it would have been able to prevent the worst of the cataclysm that engulfed the Jewish people during the Second World War. This is the truly heartbreaking thought. Indeed, if Jews had not succeeded in returning to their homeland and asserting their independence, it would be possible to see the

Holocaust as inevitable, the logical doom after centuries of abuse and oppression. But the fact that it had proved possible to return to the homeland and assert lost independence shows that the Holocaust was not a historical necessity; it was the reluctance of Jews to return to their homeland that was fatal. The proximity of the Holocaust to the creation of the state – only seven or eight years – makes the pain sometimes unbearable.

But we are celebrating what has been achieved, not what might have been. From any perspective – from a perspective of human and economic resources, from a perspective of security and local acceptance, from a perspective of geographical challenge and even international support – the last forty years began from almost nothing: a handful of people setting a national revolution in motion. However much we may criticize Israeli statesmanship – and in recent years this writer, like many of his colleagues, has certainly not spared the rod – we are compelled as human beings to feel a sense of awe. The State of Israel honours a human spirit that can create something out of nothing, that can make the wilderness bloom, and which can do so in freedom and democracy. Since 1945, Israel has restored to humanity a little of the dignity and faith that were so damaged in that most atrocious of wars.

My country will be able to preserve the spirit of its greatest achievements only if Israeli identity is felt as flesh and blood and not merely as a cloak. National identity, once so clear in the great days of Zionism, is gradually being subverted. An utterly different people also lives within Israel's borders; threats and hatred from without are no longer sufficient to guarantee solidarity, and how to hold the ranks together is increasingly problematic. Only in *Israeliness*, an identity transcending mere citizenship, can I see the guarantee of a sure and attainable future.

Recognition of Israeliness as nothing less than total Jewish identity will afford the final proof that binationality is as impossible here as it is elsewhere in the world. It will lead to the separation of two peoples whose interweaving is poisonous to both. Recognition must, however, guarantee the status of Israeli Arabs (within the Green Line borders) as a national minority with cultural and religious autonomy.

Recognition of Israeliness as total Jewish identity will inspire Jews of the free world to come and join us, in order to find what the Diaspora has taken from them.

Recognition of this identity will, I hope, dissuade Israelis from leaving the country, since to do so will mean not merely exchanging the cloak of citizenship for an equally threadbare garment of American or French origin. It will mean tearing at the very roots of personal identity.

Israeliness will restore to the Jewish people a deep awareness of its past, a past throughout which it remained closely tied to the Mediterranean on whose shores it was born. Egypt, Turkey, Greece, Jordan and Syria are our natural neighbours. Israel is not an Eastern or a Western state but a Mediterranean state, the cradle of Western culture and the vital bridge between cultures and continents.

Israelis sometimes complain that they are not judged by the same criteria as the rest of the world and are victims of overwrought moral indignation as the result. There is some truth in this charge. But Israel cannot afford to ignore the world or to be seen acting on a whim. The Jewish problem was and remains a problem for all humanity. The international community helped to create the State of Israel and its continued existence in a peaceful Middle East is an international priority. Perhaps, too, it is time for Arabs to rise above what they consider a bitter historic injustice and contribute as equal partners to the normalization of one of history's most ancient peoples. For another generation at least, the State of Israel will remain the responsibility of all mankind.

History teaches us that most *démarches*, however painful in their time, are quickly forgotten. People eventually become reconciled to new borders and are even prepared to concede land and property they have won by force of arms. But two things people are not prepared to surrender: their freedom and their identity. The Hebrew words for man (*adam*) and land (*adamah*) are very closely related, but there is a profound difference between them. Land cannot be liberated, only man can be. If anyone tries to liberate a land at the expense of another man, not only will his land not be truly liberated, he himself will lose his freedom.

But here I must conclude. I take my leave of the expert and attractive photographs of Frédéric Brenner, the French Jew. The dialogue between us has been fruitful and I am sure will continue, but the great question that I ask myself is whether my grandchildren here in Israel, forty years from now, will be able to carry on a dialogue with the grandchildren of Frédéric Brenner: will his descendants be in France, or in another country?

Haifa
January 1988

PHOTOGRAPHS ON FOLLOWING PAGES

Tahana Merkazit (Central Bus Station), Jerusalem

A falafel counter, Tel Aviv

A fan of the Maccabee-Israel basketball team

The Bedouin Market, Beer Sheva

שתו
סימן רשום

"Luna Gal" Amusement Park, the Kinneret (Sea of Galilee)

OPPOSITE From Algeria to Jerusalem: Madame Aboulker at home

ABOVE At the mud baths, Dead Sea

ספרינג
תודה
ולהתראות
HACKS

OPPOSITE A *makolet* (grocery store), Jerusalem

ABOVE The power station, Hadera

BELOW With Rabbi Lelov at *Avdallah* (the ceremony at the close of the Sabbath), Jerusalem

OPPOSITE The Jewess from Yemen, Ballet Inbal

OPPOSITE Eliyahou Ben Raphael Sidi, painter and sculptor, En Karem, Jerusalem

ABOVE Traditional folk dancing from Bukhara at a wedding reception

OPPOSITE *Mimouna* (the festival at the close of Passover)

BELOW Beit Daniel music workshop, Zikhron Ya'akov

אסור לעשן

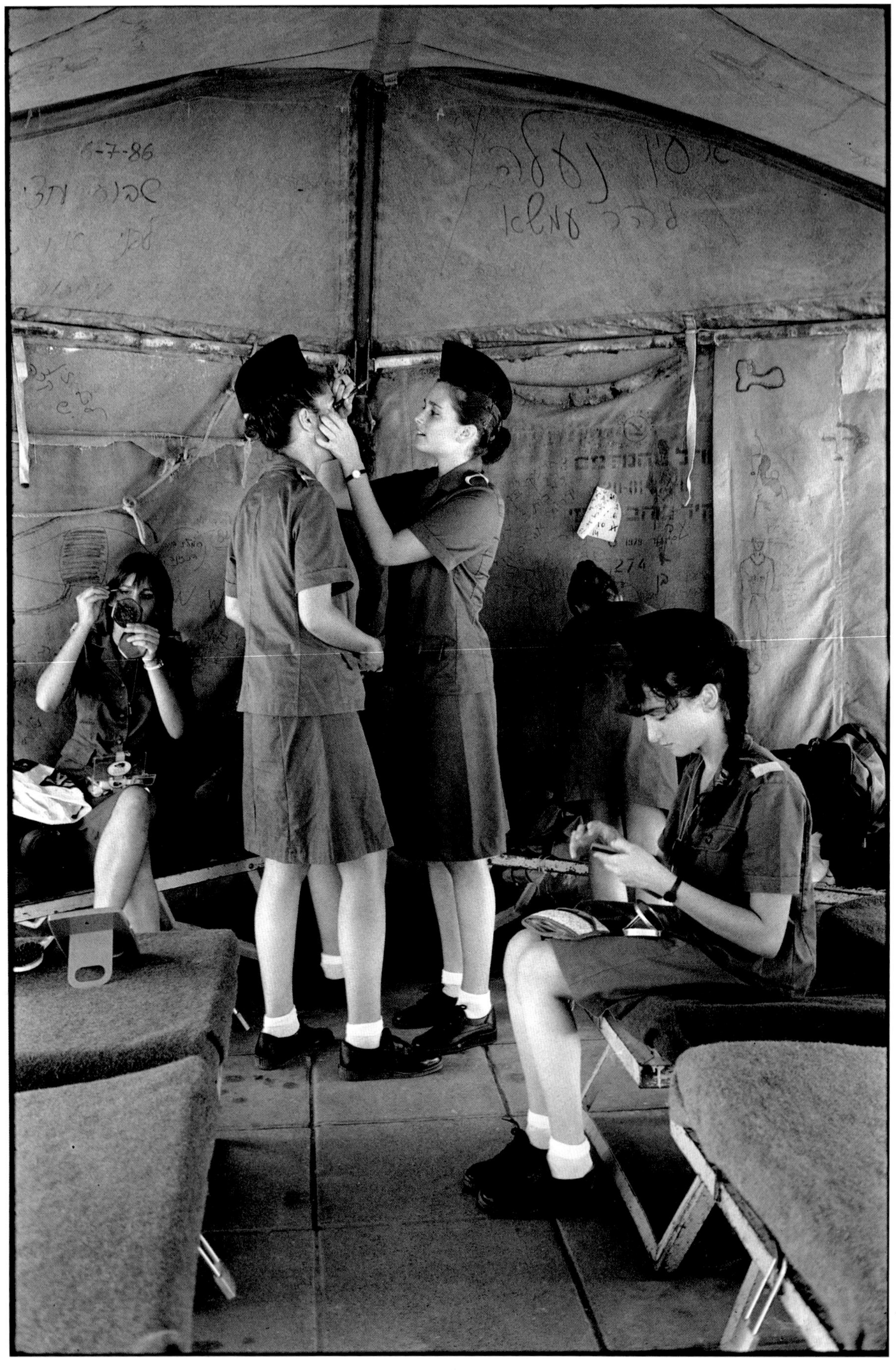

OPPOSITE Young conscripts before their Passing Out parade

ABOVE A ballet workshop, Hadassim

ABOVE Fond farewells at the end of summer camp

OPPOSITE The funeral of a young officer, twenty-two years old, killed in Gaza

PHOTOGRAPHS ON FOLLOWING PAGES

Pages 108–109 Jerusalem, from the Judaean Desert

Pages 110–111 The Western Wall and Temple Mount, Jerusalem

OPPOSITE The Western Wall, Tishab b'Ab 5746 (the day of mourning marking the destruction of the Temple), Jerusalem

BELOW Russian Orthodox Sisters, Good Friday, Via Dolorosa, Jerusalem

Purim (the Feast of Esther), Jerusalem

ABOVE Pilgrims at prayer, with postcard seller, Via Dolorosa, Jerusalem
OPPOSITE The market, Muslim Quarter, Old City, Jerusalem

In the Muslim Quarter, Old City, Jerusalem

A news stand, Haifa

ABOVE AND OPPOSITE Tel Aviv

OVERLEAF Tel Aviv: the city from Jaffa

המועצה לארץ ישראל יפה
PAZ
נפט
פז
PAZ
פז
נפט

5
רח' הִלֵּל הַזָּקֵן
מגדולי התנאים הראשונים, אבי שושלת הנשיאים
מבית הלל, חי כמאה שנה לפני החורבן
REHOV HILLEL HAZAKEN
רח' הלל הזקן 5
טל.

OPPOSITE A barber's shop, Tel Aviv

ABOVE Sderot Nordau, Tel Aviv

Ethiopian Jews at the *Merkaz Klita* (reception centre for new immigrants), Hadera

Merkaz Klita, Hadera

OPPOSITE The university campus, Tel Aviv

BELOW 6 a.m., Tel Aviv

LEFT The Synagogue, Hebrew University, Mount Scopus, Jerusalem

BELOW Arieh Hakadosch Synagogue, Safed

OPPOSITE From a Byzantine frieze, Qasrin Museum, Golan Heights

ABOVE The Weizmann Institute, Rehovot

ABOVE A billboard, near Haifa

OPPOSITE A fragment of the Book of Isaiah, one of the Dead Sea Scrolls in the Shrine of the Book, Jerusalem

BELOW Menashe Kadishman, painter and sculptor

OPPOSITE Yeshayahou Leibowitz, philosopher and scientist

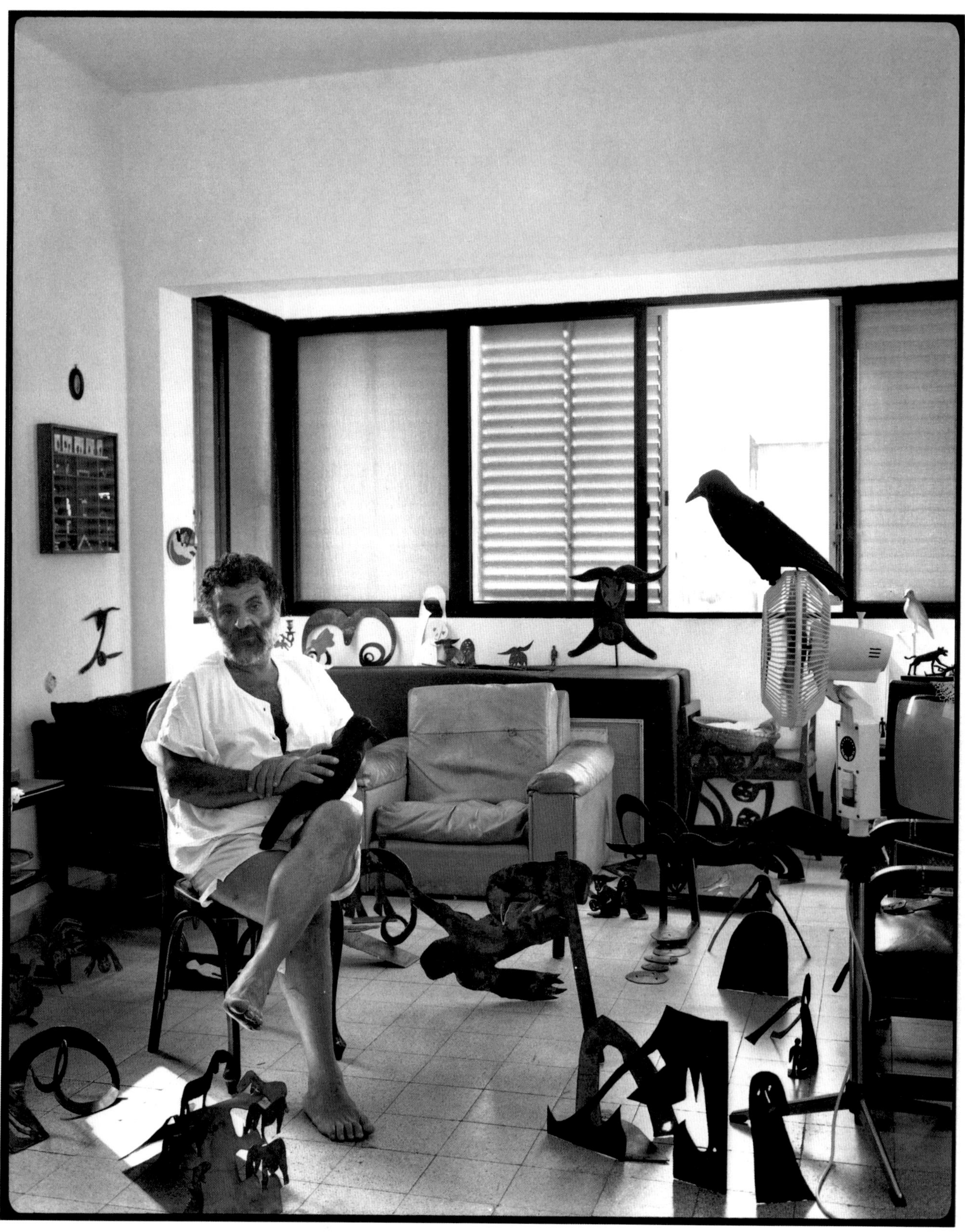

PHOTOGRAPHS ON PRECEDING PAGES

Pages 140–141 The Kinneret (Sea of Galilee)

Pages 142–143 The Jordan Valley

Pages 144–145 The Mountains of Moab, from near Mount Sodom, Dead Sea

ABOVE The Negev–Sinai border, near Eilat

OPPOSITE The Greek Orthodox Monastery of Mar Saba, Judaean Desert

ABOVE A summer camp in the Negev
OPPOSITE Akko (St Jean d'Acre)

ABOVE Potash wagons *en route* from Dimona to Ashdod in the Negev

OPPOSITE On manoeuvres in the Negev

ABOVE New immigrants to Israel begin military conscription

OPPOSITE A civilian army: reporting for the first day of annual reserve service

From the Theatre of Haifa's performance of *The Palestinian* by Yehoshua Sobol

In a military telecommunications bunker, Golan Heights

ABOVE Customs control, Allenby Bridge on the Jordanian border

OPPOSITE An identity check, Gaza

BELOW In the Gaza Strip

OPPOSITE Rami Fields, with his Jewish-Israeli foreman and Arab labourers on the site of a new house, Jerusalem

BELOW Near Bethlehem

OPPOSITE Picnickers, Tel Aviv

RIGHT Samaria

OPPOSITE In Kiryat Shemona

BELOW Bedouin, near Beer Sheva

OPPOSITE On the Mount of Olives, Jerusalem

ABOVE Dizengoff Street, 10 a.m., Friday, Tel Aviv

OPPOSITE Marching against the cancellation of the Lavi fighter, Jerusalem

מה מבין...
תנו סיכוי
לעתיד
טוב יותר

A waitress, Bar Herzl,
Tel Aviv

OPPOSITE Kibbutz Bar'am,
Upper Galilee

"Black" Jews, Mea Shearim, Jerusalem

BELOW The children's quarters, Kibbutz Bar'am, Upper Galilee

OPPOSITE Showering after work, a mineral plant, Dead Sea

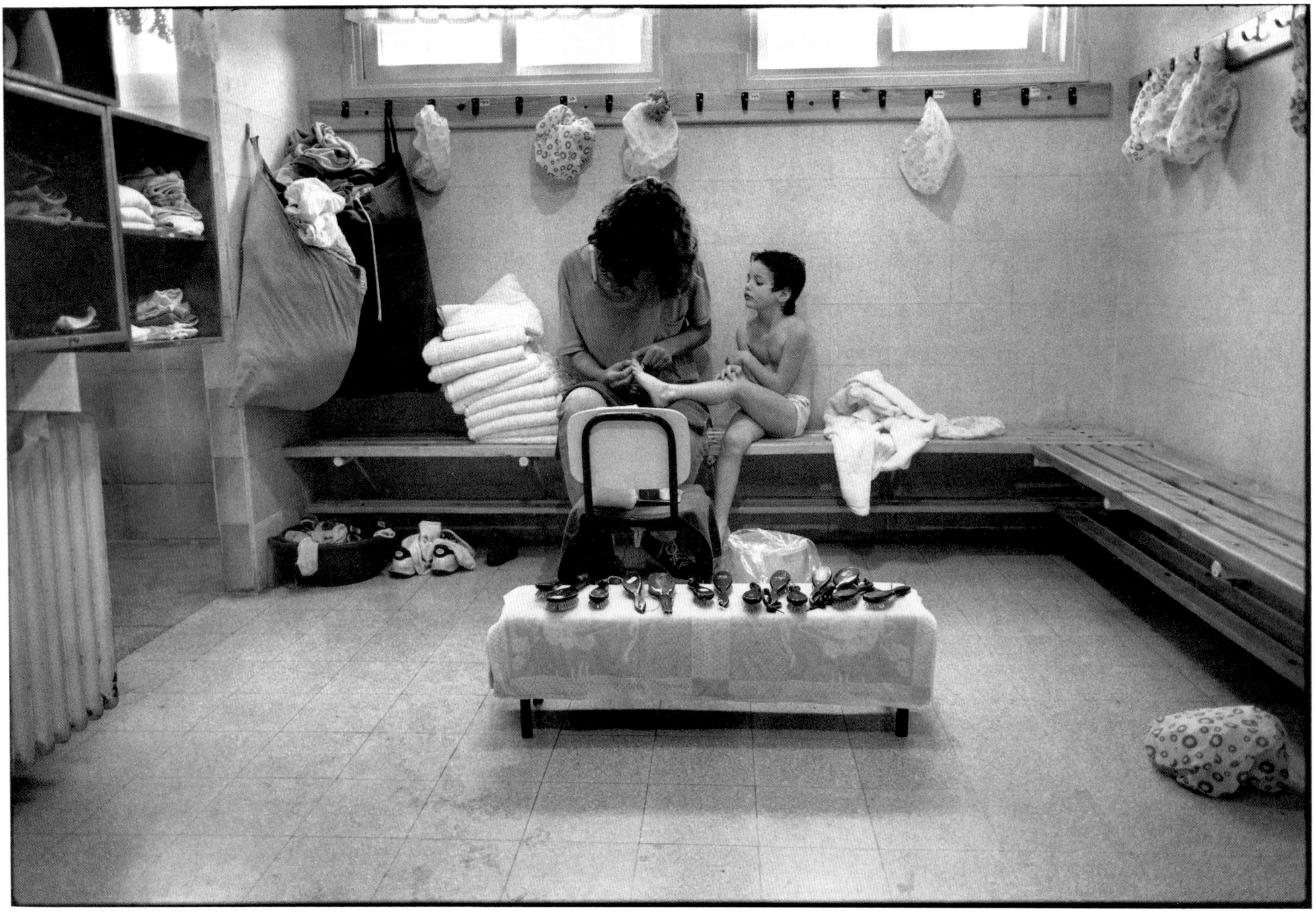

Towards Talpiot Mizrach, Jerusalem

A courtyard, Mea Shearim, Jerusalem

A new Jewish settlement, the West Bank

BELOW A State Nurse, on her rounds, in a Bedouin household

OPPOSITE A Druse family, Jatt, Lower Galilee

Mohamed Abou Marouan, an Arab Israeli, with his wife and family, Akko (St Jean d'Acre)

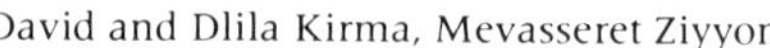

David and Dlila Kirma, Mevasseret Ziyyon

Ouzi and Rama Ben-Zi, Nataf, near Abu Gosh

Mr Zimmerman, who survived the Holocaust and is now a successful industrialist, with his wife and daughter, Kefar Shmaryaou, Herzliyya

A young religious family in their new apartment, West Bank

Nissim Chochani, originally from Morocco, with his Polish-Israeli wife, their sons and daughter, Moshav Givat Yoav, Golan Heights

LEFT Sledding, Mount Hermon

BELOW The crèche, Kibbutz Mizpe Shalem, near the Dead Sea

ACKNOWLEDGEMENTS

I am extremely grateful to the many people and organizations who helped me in the preparation of this book. In particular I should like to thank Moria and Marga Kaplan, Edna Bar Romi, Beverly Gordey, Guila Toledano, Said El Sana, Nissim Chochani, Doron Bachar, Nissim Kripsi, Ralph Horowitz, David Kreyselman; as also Dover Tsahal, Shulamit Davara of the Israeli Ministry of Foreign Affairs, Yael Shoam of the Hevera Lehaganah Hate'va, the Israel Museum, Jerusalem, for permission to reproduce the fragment of the Book of Isaiah on page 137, Emile Savoye of Ilford France, M. Devley of Fuji Film France who very kindly lent me the camera equipment with which I was able to take the panoramic landscape photographs, and Pierre and Eddy Gassman of Pictorial.

I owe a great debt to David Zilber of Beth Hatefutsoth (the Nahum Goldmann Museum of the Jewish Diaspora), without whose encouragement and advice this book would not have been possible, and to Jerome Stern, Andy and Charles Bronfman and Mr and Mrs Leywcovitz. Finally, I must thank my wife, Miriam, for her patience and understanding during the long months of travel and preparation.

FREDERIC BRENNER

PHOTOGRAPHS ON PRECEDING PAGES

Pages 186–187 Morning prayers, with troops from the *Yeshiva Esder*, a unit combining religious studies with military service, Judaea

Pages 188–189 The Zin Negev, near En Avdat

Pages 190–191 Temple Mount and the Old City from the Mount of Olives, Jerusalem